SPPU New Syllabus

COMPUTER CONCEPTS AND APPLICATIONS - II

for

First Year B.Com. Semester - II

CBCS Pattern [Course Code 124-B]

As Per New Syllabus, June 2019

Prof. Gautam Bapat

Program Head BBA (Global e-Business)
B.Sc., MCA, PGDBM (Marketing), MMS (Marketing)
Asst. Professor, Computer Science & Applications, Marketing
MIT World Peace University, Pune

Dr. D. P. Kotkar

M.C.M., M.Com., M.Phil., Ph.D.
Professor, Commerce Dept.,
Prof. Ramkrishna More Arts, Com., Sci. College
Akurdi, Pune 44

NIRALI PRAKASHAN
ADVANCEMENT OF KNOWLEDGE

N5122

Computer Concepts & Applications - II **ISBN 978-93-89686-55-5**
First Edition : December 2019

Published By:
NIRALI PRAKASHAN
Abhyudaya Pragati, 1312, Shivaji Nagar
Off J.M. Road, PUNE – 411005
Tel - (020) 25512336/37/39, Fax - (020) 25511379
Email : niralipune@pragationline.com

➢ DISTRIBUTION CENTRES

PUNE

Nirali Prakashan (For orders within Pune) : 119, Budhwar Peth, Jogeshwari Mandir Lane, Pune 411002, Maharashtra, Tel : (020) 2445 2044, Mobile : 9657703145
Email : niralilocal@pragationline.com

Nirali Prakashan (For orders outside Pune) : S. No. 28/27, Dhayari, Near Asian College Pune 411041
Tel : (020) 24690204; Mobile : 9657703143
Email : bookorder@pragationline.com

MUMBAI

Nirali Prakashan : 385, S.V.P. Road, Rasdhara Co-op. Hsg. Society Ltd., Girgaum, Mumbai 400004, Maharashtra;
Mobile : 9320129587 Tel : (022) 2385 6339 / 2386 9976,
Fax : (022) 2386 9976
Email : niralimumbai@pragationline.com

➢ DISTRIBUTION BRANCHES

JALGAON

Nirali Prakashan : 34, V. V. Golani Market, Navi Peth, Jalgaon 425001, Maharashtra, Tel : (0257) 222 0395, Mob : 94234 91860;
Email : niralijalgaon@pragationline.com

KOLHAPUR

Nirali Prakashan : New Mahadvar Road, Kedar Plaza, 1st Floor Opp. IDBI Bank, Kolhapur 416 012, Maharashtra. Mob : 9850046155;
Email : niralikolhapur@pragationline.com

NAGPUR

Nirali Prakashan : Above Maratha Mandir, Shop No. 3, First Floor, Rani Jhanshi Square, Sitabuldi, Nagpur 440012, Maharashtra
Tel : (0712) 254 7129;
Email : niralinagpur@pragationline.com

DELHI

Nirali Prakashan : 4593/15, Basement, Agarwal Lane, Ansari Road, Daryaganj Near Times of India Building, New Delhi 110002
Mob : 08505972553, Email : niralidelhi@pragationline.com

BENGALURU

Nirali Prakashan : Maitri Ground Floor, Jaya Apartments, No. 99, 6th Cross, 6th Main, Malleswaram, Bengaluru 560003, Karnataka;
Mob : 9449043034
Email: niralibangalore@pragationline.com

Other Branches : Hyderabad, Chennai

niralipune@pragationline.com | www.pragationline.com

Also find us on f www.facebook.com/niralibooks

Preface ...

We take an opportunity to present this book entitled as "Computer Concepts and Applications - II" to the students of First Year B. Com. The object of this book is to present the subject matter in a most concise and simple manner. The book is written strictly according to the New Syllabus of Savitribai Phule Pune University.

The book has its own unique features. It brings out the subject in a very simple and lucid manner for easy and comprehensive understanding of the basic concepts, its intricacies, procedures and practices. This book will help the readers to have a broader view on Computer Fundamentals. The language used in this book is easy and will help students to improve their vocabulary of Technical terms and understand the matter in a better and happier way.

We sincerely thank Shri. Dineshbhai Furia and Shri. Jignesh Furia, the publishers, for the confidence reposed in us and giving us this opportunity to reach out to the students of commerce studies.

We thank Mrs. Anita Panajkar, Prajakta, Madhuri for their important inputs time to time. Mr. Akbar Shaikh painstakingly attended to all the details to make this book appear good.

We also thank Ms. Chaitali Takale, Mr. Ravindra Walodare, Mr. Sachin Shinde, Nikunj Joshi, Nilesh Deshmukh, Ashok Bodke, Moshin Sayyed and Nitin Thorat.

We have given our best inputs for this book. Any suggestions towards the improvement of this book and sincere comments are most welcome on niralipune@pragationline.com.

PUNE **AUTHORS**

December 2019

■■■

Syllabus ...

Unit 1 : Introduction to E-commerce Tools [12]

Process of E-Commerce

Types of E-Commerce; Role of Internet and Web in E-Commerce; Technologies Used in E-Commerce Systems.

E-Commerce Activities:

Various Activities of E-Commerce; Various Modes of Operation Associated with E-Commerce; Elements and Resources Impacting E-Commerce and Changes; Types of E-Commerce Providers and Vendors; Opportunity Development for E-Commerce Stages; Development of E-Commerce Business Case; Components and Factors for the Development of The Business Case; Steps To Design and Develop and E-Commerce Website.

Unit 2 : Introductions to E-Marketing [14]

E-Marketing:

Traditional Marketing; E-Marketing; Identifying Web Presence Goals – Achieving Web Presence Goals, Uniqueness of The Web, Meeting The Needs of Website Visitors, Site Adhesion: Content, Format and Access; Maintaining a Website; Metrics Defining Internet Units of Measurement; Online Marketing; Advantages of Online Marketing.

E-Customer Relationship Management:

Customer Relationship Management (CRM) – Marketing Automation, Enterprise Customer Management; Customer Relationship Management Areas; CRM Processes, Architectural Components of a CRM Solution – Customer's Information Repository, Campaign Management, Event triggers, Business Logic and Rules Repository, Forecasting and Planning Tools, Electronic Customer Relationship Management; Need Architecture and Applications of Electronic CRM.

Supply Chain Management:

Supply Chain Management (SCM); Goals of SCM; Functions of SCM; Strategies of SCM; Electronic SCM and its benefits; Components of Electronic SCM; Electronic Logistics and its Implementation.

Unit 3 : Electronic Payment System [14]

Electronic Data Interchange (Introduction to EDI, EDI Architecture Financial EDI, Overview of the technology involved in EDI).

Introduction to EPS

Application of Online Payment System, Introduction to EFT (Electronic Fund Transfer) Types of EFT (NEFT, RTGS), E-Payment Systems: Electronic Funds Transfer; Digital Token Based E-Payment Systems; Modern Payment Systems; Steps for Electronic Payment; Payment Security; Net Banking. Introduction to Digital Signature and Digital Certificates, Stages of SET. Types of Payment System: Digital Cash, Electronic Cheque, Smart Card, Credit/Debit Card.

Unit 4 : Introduction to M-Commerce [8]

Definition, Need and Scope, Advantages and Disadvantages of M-Commerce, M-Commerce and its Applications. Types of M-Commerce, Products and Services of M-Commerce. Mobile Payment Application. Difference between E-Commerce and M-Commerce.

■■■

Contents ...

■■■

Unit 1...

Introduction to E-Commerce Tools

Objectives ...

- To understand process of E-Commerce.
- To get knowledge about E-Commerce Activities.

1.1 INTRODUCTION

- E-Commerce is currently one of the most important aspects of the Internet. The term Electronic commerce refers to the use of an electronic medium to carry out commercial transactions.
- E-Commerce, (Electronic Commerce), is online commerce verses real-world commerce. E-Commerce described as buying and selling of goods/products and services over the Internet.
- The potential dimension of E-Commerce today is the considerable cost savings that could occur if a company's business is done electronically.
- E-Commerce involves in advertising, multimedia, product information, customer support on the World Wide Web (WWW), internet security and payment mechanism are all covered under electronic commerce.

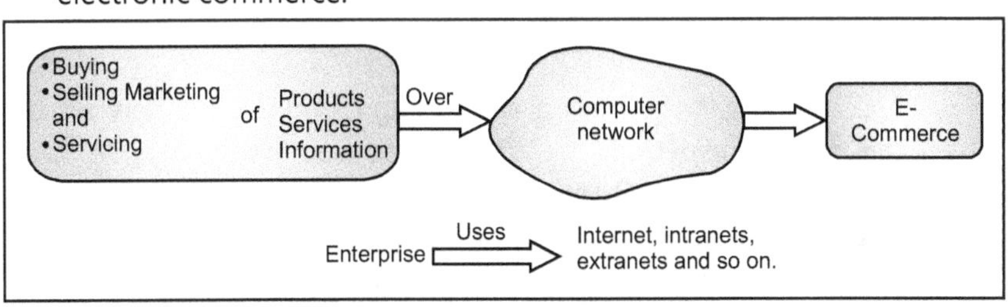

Fig. 1.1: E-Commerce basic design

- Electronic Commerce include following examples:
  - Use of multimedia web pages of product catalogs on the internet.

- Use by sales representatives to access customer records through corporate intranet.
- Access of inventory databases by large customers through the extranet.

- E-Commerce covers a range of different types of businesses, from consumer based retail sites, through auction or music sites, to business exchanges trading goods and services between corporations.
- E-Commerce includes retail shopping, banking, stocks and bonds trading, auctions, real estate transactions, airline booking, movie rentals, nearly anything which can imagine in the real world.

1.1.1 Definition of E-Commerce

- Some of the definitions of E-Commerce often heard and found in publications and the media are listed below:
  - Doing business online is known as E-Commerce.

OR

  - Electronic Commerce (EC) is where business transactions take place via telecommunications networks, especially the internet.

OR

  - Electronic Commerce describes the buying and selling of products, services, and information via computer networks including the internet.

OR

  - Electronic Commerce is about doing business electronically.

OR

  - E-Commerce or Electronic Commerce is defined as the conduct of a financial transaction by electronic means.

OR

  - E-Commerce is the buying and selling of goods and services on the internet, especially the World Wide Web (www).

1.1.2 Advantages of E-Commerce

- The benefits of E-Commerce can be seen to affect three major stakeholders: organizations, consumers and society.

1. **Advantages of E-Commerce to Organisations:**

   (i) International marketplace: Using E-Commerce, organizations can expand their market to national and international markets with minimum capital investment. An organization can easily locate more customers, best suppliers, and suitable business partners across the globe.

(ii) **Saves Operational cost:** The cost of creating, processing, distributing, storing and retrieving paper-based information has decreased.

(iii) **Mass customization:** E-Commerce has transformed the way consumers buy goods and services. The "Pull" type processing allows for products and services to be customised to the customer's requirements.

In the past when Ford first started making motor cars, customers could have any colour so long as it was black. Now customers can configure a car according to their specifications within minutes online via the www.ford.com website.

(iv) **Reduced inventories and overheads:** E-Commerce increases the productivity of organizations. It supports "pull" type supply management. In "pull" type supply management, a business process starts when a request comes from a customer and it uses just-in-time manufacturing way.

For example, companies like Motorola (mobile phones), and Dell (computers) collect customer orders for a product, transmit them electronically to the manufacturing plant. In these plants they are manufactured according to the customer's specifications (like colour and features) and then sent to the customer within a few days.

(v) **Lower telecommunications cost:** The internet is much cheaper than Value Added Networks (VANs) which were based on leased telephone lines. It is also cheaper to send a fax or e-mail via the internet than direct dialing.

(vi) **Digitisation of products and processes:** Software and music/video products can be downloaded or e-mailed directly to customers via the internet in digital or electronic format.

(vii) **No more 24-hour-time constraints:** Businesses can be contacted at any time.

2. **Advantages of E-Commerce to Consumers:**

(i) **24/7 access:** Enables customers to shop or conduct other transactions 24 hours a day, all year round from almost any location. For example, checking balances, making payments, obtaining travel and other information.

(ii) **More choices:** E-Commerce application provides users with more options and quicker delivery of products.

(iii) **Price comparisons:** E-Commerce application provides users with more options to compare and select the cheaper and better options.

(iv) **Improved delivery processes:** This can range from the immediate delivery of digitised or electronic goods such as software or audio-visual files by downloading via internet, to the online tracking of the progress of packages being delivered by mail or courier.

(v) **An environment of competition:** E-Commerce increases the competition among organizations and as a result, organizations provides useful discounts to customers.

Advantages of E-Commerce to Society:

1. **Enables more flexible working practices:**

(i) **E-Commerce provides advantages to the society:** E-Commerce provides more individuals work at home. This reduces traveling for work which results in less air pollution and less traffic on the roads.

(ii) **Connects people:** Using E-Commerce, some merchandise can be sold at lower prices. That can allow less wealthy people to buy more and increase standard of living. People in developing countries and rural areas can be able to enjoy products and services that were unavailable in the past.

(iii) **Facilitates delivery of public services:** Public services, such as health care, education, and distribution of government social services, can be done at a reduced cost and/or improved quality.

1.1.3 Disadvantages of E-Commerce

1. **Disadvantages of E-Commerce to Organisations:**

(i) **Lack of system security:** There are numerous reports of websites and databases being hacked into, and security holes in software. For example, Microsoft has over the years issued many security notices and 'patches' for their software.

(ii) **Rapidly changing technology:** Because of rapidly evolving and changing technology, there is always a feeling of trying to 'catch up' and not be left behind.

(iii) **Under pressure to innovate and develop business models** to develop the new opportunities which sometimes leads to strategies harmful to the organisation. The ease with which business models can be copied and emulated over the internet increase the pressure and restrict longer-term competitive advantage.

(iv) **Facing increased competition:** From both national and international competitors often leads to price wars and subsequent unsustainable losses for the organisation.

(v) **Problems with compatibility of older and newer technology:** There could be software/hardware compatibility issues, as some E-Commerce software may be incompatible with some operating system or any other component.

2. **Disadvantages of E-Commerce to Consumers:**

(i) Computing equipment is needed for individuals to participate in the new digital economy, which means an initial capital cost to customers.

(ii) A basic technical knowledge is required for both computing equipment and navigation of the internet and the World Wide Web (www).

(iii) Cost of access to the internet, whether dial-up or broadband tariffs.

(iv) Cost of computing equipment, not just the initial cost of buying equipment but making sure that the technology is updated regularly to be compatible with the changing requirement of the internet, websites and applications.

(v) Lack of security and privacy of personal data, there is no real control of data that is collected over the web or internet. Data protection laws are not universal and so websites hosted in different countries may or may not have laws which protect privacy of personal data.

(vi) Physical contact and relationships are replaced by electronic processes, customers are unable to touch and feel goods being sold online or display voices and reactions of human beings.

(vii) A lack of trust because they are interacting with faceless computers.

3. **Disadvantages of E-Commerce to Society:**

(i) **Lack of personal touch:** It is kind of consumer feeling that consumer can't feel and touch the product. Sometimes no matter how good a product is explained and expressed you will not be able to sense the touch, smell, taste, and sound, through the dimensionality of a screen. This is what makes E-Commerce sometimes in a situation where customer faces bit trust issues over products.

(ii) **Social division:** There is a potential danger that there will be an increase in the social division between technical haves and have-nots – so people who do not have technical skills become unable to secure better-paid jobs and could form an underclass with potentially dangerous implications for social stability.

(iii) **Reliance on telecommunications infrastructure**, power and IT skills, which in developing countries nullifies the benefits when power, advanced telecommunication infrastructures and IT skills are unavailable or insufficient or underdeveloped.

(iv) **Wasted resources:** As new technology updates quickly there arises a problem of disposing all the old computers, keyboards, monitors, speakers and other hardware or software.

(v) **Takes time for the ordered item to arrive at your home:** When you go shopping at the supermarket, you can bring the item with you at the same day you buy it. In E-Commerce, you must wait for a several days before you really can use the product. Even with the fastest shipping option, you still have to wait for several hours.

(vi) **Difficulty in policing the Internet:** Numerous crimes can be committed and often go undetected.

1.1.4 Types of E-Commerce

- E-Commerce categories represent a range of various schemas of transactions which are distinguished according to their participants. Usually E-Commerce is divided into three general most well-known types, but the concept is much wider.

  Following are types of E-Commerce:

1. **B2B (Business to Business):**

- Now-a-days B2B is considered as one of the most perspective and extensively developing E-Commerce trend. It refers to Electronic Commerce between businesses and also supplies chain technology, which is the largest and most successful E-Commerce technology nowadays.

- The parties of B2B schema are Business Partners. Internet platforms give an opportunity to considerably simplify all steps of the operations, make the trade more immediate.
- An example of B2B schema is selling site templates to companies for using as a design base, besides any other interactions involving bulk deliveries are included.
- B2B means an established working relationship therefore it is a better solution to deliver comparing to B2C, although it needs to link together two complex accounting systems.
- B2B E-Commerce is simply defined as E-Commerce between companies. About 80% of E-Commerce is of this type.

Fig. 1.2: B2B E-Commerce model

Examples:

- Intel selling microprocessor to Dell.
- Heinz selling ketchup to Mc Donalds.

2. B2C (Business to Consumer):

- B2C has lately gained a big popularity due to simplified and accelerated way to buy products.
- Business to Consumer refers to selling and buying of goods and services via the web. The parties are: a company (a web retailer) who trades to an individual (a web customer).
- Retail trading (via online shops) is the most well-known example of such type of transactions. In this trading, allowing consumers to purchase by lower prices and with more convenience.
- The disadvantages of B2C E-Commerce type are selling to un-trusted strangers and extra effort to get customer and payment information. However, B2C almost always involves a customer typing information into an order screen therefore it is a better solution to provide comparing to B2B.

- Business-to-Consumer E-Commerce or commerce between companies and consumers, involves customers collecting information; purchasing physical goods or receiving products over an electronic network.

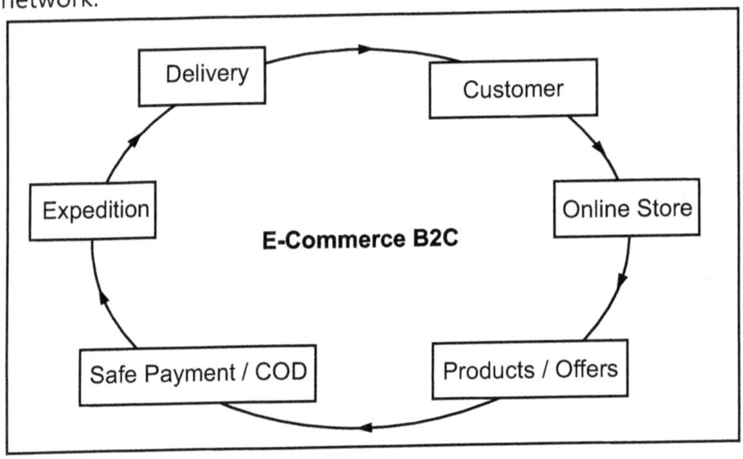

Fig. 1.3: B2C E-Commerce model

Examples:

- Dell selling a laptop to customer.

3. **C2C (Consumer to Consumer):**

- C2C refers to online dealing of goods and services between people. The parties are two consumers (individuals).
- This type of transaction is fulfilled due to online market dealer like auction sites, becoming more and more popular nowadays (for example eBay).
- Consumer-to-Consumer E-Commerce or C2C is simply commerce between private individuals or consumers.

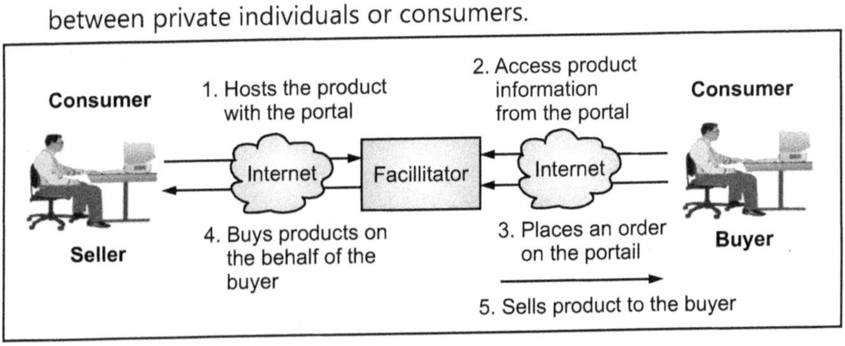

Fig. 1.4: C2C E-Commerce model

Examples:

- Alia buying an iPod from Jui on eBay.
- Ayush selling a car to his neighbour.

4. **C2B (Consumer to Business)**:

- C2B is growing trend where consumers demand specific products or services from respective businesses by presenting themselves as a buyer group.

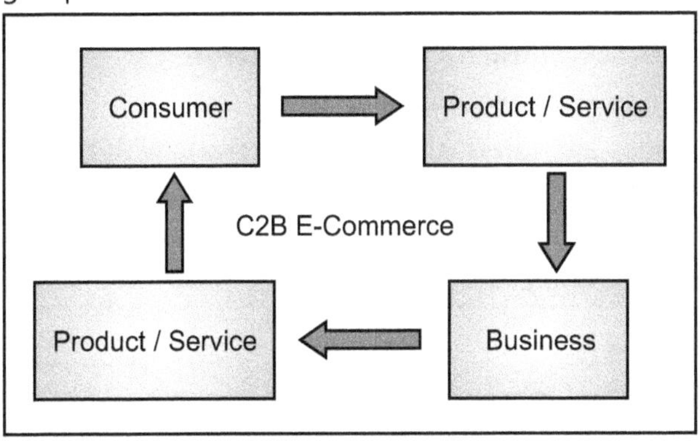

Fig. 1.5: C2B E-Commerce model

- Example of this type is contacting a tour and travel operator via their website for purchasing a holiday package as well as such sites as CTB and SpeakOut.com. These sites provide consumers with market strategies. They are also used by businesses to gain insight into consumer wants.

5. **Business-to-Government (B2G):**

- B2G is the exchange of information, services and products between business organisations and government agencies online. This may include:
  - E-procurement services, in which businesses learn about the purchasing needs of agencies and provide services.
  - A virtual workplace in which a business and a government agency could co-ordinate the work on a contracted project by collaborating online to co-ordinate online meetings, review plans and manage progress.
  - Rental of online applications and databases designed especially for use by government agencies.

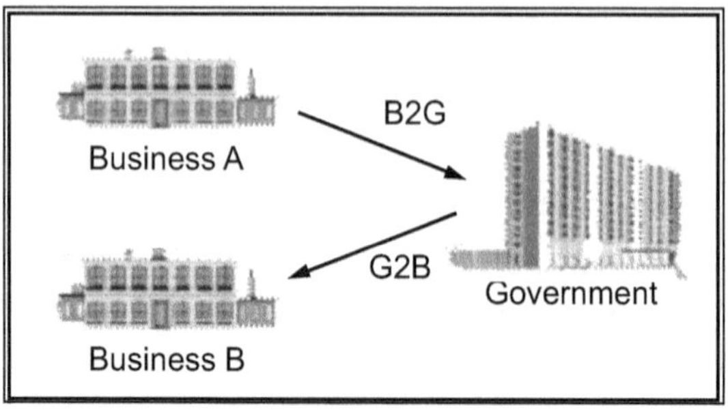

Fig. 1.6: B2G E-Commerce

6. Consumer-to-Government (C2G):

- In this model, an individual customer interacts with the Government. For example, a consumer can pay online his income tax or house tax.
- C2G transactions where consumers provide services to government have yet to be implemented.

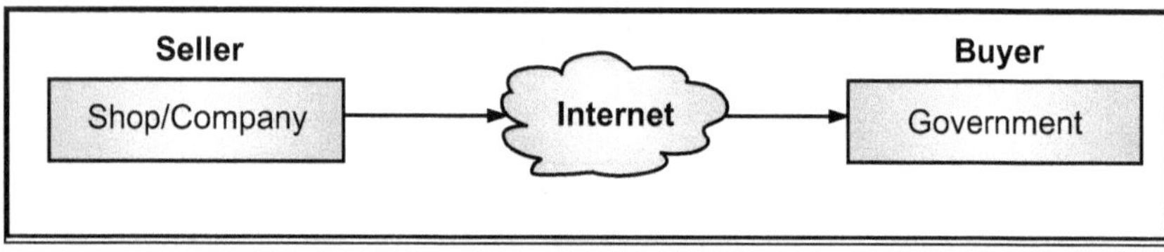

Fig. 1.7: C2G E-Commerce

7. Business-to-Administration (B2A):

- The Business-to-Administration (B2A) category covers all online transactions between companies and public administration. This domain encompasses a large number and range of services, namely in the fiscal, social security, employment, registries and notary areas, etc.
- Although still in its early stages of development, B2A is bound to grow rapidly, particularly due to public administrations promotion of electronic commerce and the latest developments in e-government.

8. Consumer-to-Administration (C2A):

- The Consumer-to-Administration model encompasses all electronic transactions conducted between individuals and public administration.
- Examples of applications include:
  - Education – distributing information, distance learning, etc.
  - Social Security – through the distribution of information, making payments, etc.

- Taxes – filing tax returns, payments, etc.
- Health – appointments, information about illnesses, payment of health services, etc.

* Both models involving Public Administration (B2A and C2A) are strongly associated to the idea of efficiency and easy usability of the services provided to citizens by the government, with the support of information and communication technologies.

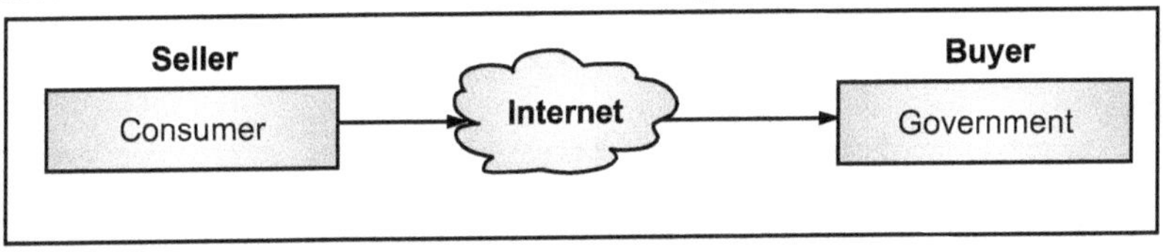

Fig. 1.8: C2A E-Commerce Model

9. Peer–to-Peer (P2P):

* P2P is the communications model in which each party has the same capabilities and either party can initiate a communication session.
* Peer-to-peer technology enables Internet users to share files and computer resources directly without having to go through a central web server.
* The focus in P2P companies is on helping individuals make information available for anyone's use by connecting users on the web.
* For example: Napster.com, which was established to aid Internet users in finding and sharing online music files.
* P2P is a technology in itself which helps people to directly share computer files and computer resources without having to go through a central web server. To use this, both sides need to install the required software so that they can communicate on the common platform. This type of E-Commerce has quite low revenue generation as from the beginning it has been inclined to the free usage due to which it sometimes got entangled in cyber laws.
* In recent usage, peer-to-peer has come to describe applications in which users can use the Internet to exchange files with each other directly or through a mediating server.

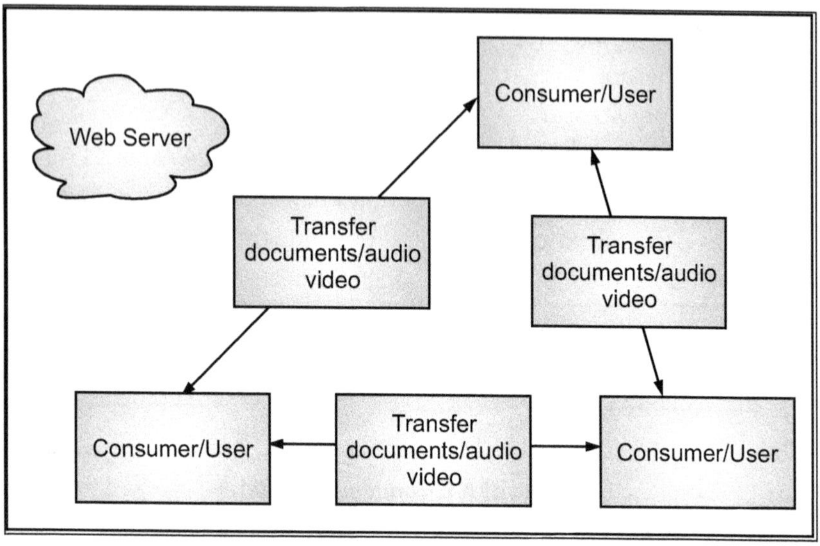

Fig. 1.9: Peer to Peer E-Commerce Model

1.1.5 Role of Internet and Web in E-Commerce

- The Internet and its underlying technologies provide the infrastructure of E-Commerce.
- Web and networking technologies that include TCP/IP Protocols, Web Servers, Cloud computing and the mobile platform enable large amount of E-Commerce applications. Online Shopping Carts, Supply Chain Management and Customer Relationship Management applications are some of the systems made possible by the development of the Internet.
- Following are some important roles of Internet and web in E-Commerce.
  - **Selling Products:** Internet helps business and E-Commerce website to automate selling and transactions process. Selling products via the online store is not only beneficial for one business but it helps third-party business services such as couriers, content marketers, graphic designers, payment gateway service providers, etc.
  - **Advertisement:** The Internet plays an important role to advertise & market products and services around the world to get more customers. The business organization is using high-speed internet to speed up the production.

- **Marketing:** Internet technology provides powerful communication and marketing tools. The Internet is a new Bazaar in which you can find online shops, online degree programs and a lot more. You can browse various educational and business development websites, management service platforms anytime & anywhere.
- **Review:** Internet helps businesses to test and collect the data behind the idea of product and services.
- **Training:** Online employee training and web-based training programs are providing great benefits to manage and execute tasks effectively.
- **Communication:** Internet helps the business to connect with customer's communication channels and build a strong network. Communication by Internet platforms helps the business to get new customers and retain existing customers.
- **Data access:** The World Wide Web gives you access to data and information with high speed and accuracy. Emails, News, file transfers, cloud storage, Internet Relay Chat (IRC) such kind of Internet features are really important for the business.

1.1.6 Technologies used in E-Commerce Systems

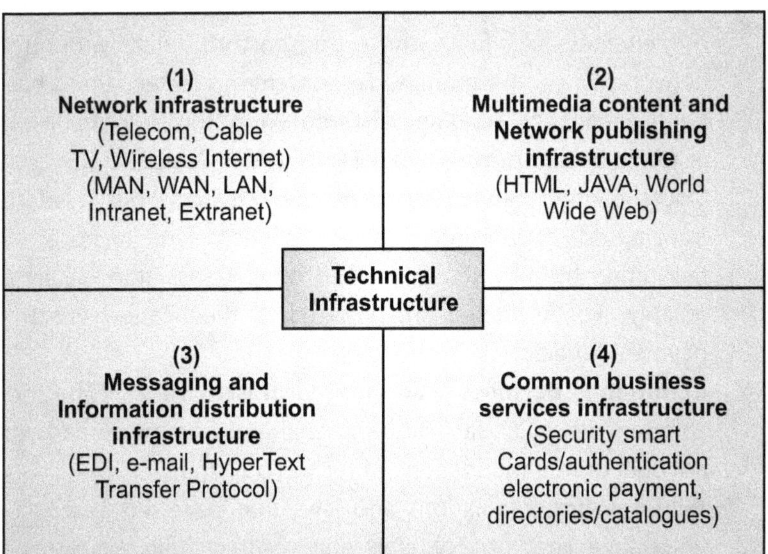

Fig. 1.10: Technologies used in E-Commerce Systems

- The technological foundations of E-Commerce are largely hidden, but they are the base on which Electronic Commerce is built.
  1. **Network Infrastructure** is like the network of roads that are interconnected and are of different widths, lengths and quality. For example: internet, local area networks, intranets.

     Network infrastructures also take different forms such as telephone wires, cables, wireless technology, such as satellite or cellular technology etc.
  2. **The Publishing Infrastructure** (including the World Wide Web, Web servers) can be seen as the infrastructure of vehicles and warehouses, which store and transport electronic data and multimedia content along the network.

     Multimedia Content is created using myriad tools such as HTML and JAVA. This content can be very different with varying degrees of complexity similar to different vehicles travelling on the roads.

     For example, text only, or more complex is an application, such as a computer game, containing audio, video, graphics and a programme.
  3. **Messaging and Information Distribution Infrastructure** are the engines and fuel, which transport the data around the network. Once, the multimedia content is created, there has to be a means of sending and retrieving this information, for example by EDI, e-mail, Hyper Text Transfer Protocol.

     Once content and data can be created, displayed and transmitted supporting business services are necessary for facilitating the buying, selling and other transactions safely and reliably. For example, smart cards, authentication, electronic payment, directories/ catalogues.
  4. **Common Business Service Infrastructure**: The next components which facilitate and enable E-Commerce and which are built on the foundations of technology are:

     Public policy, regulations and laws that govern issues such as universal access, privacy, electronic contracts and the terms and conditions that govern E-Commerce.

Universal agreement of technical standards dictate the format in which electronic data is transferred over networks and is received across user interfaces, and the format in which it is stored. This is necessary so that data can travel seamlessly across different networks, where information and data can be accessed by a whole range of hardware and software such as computers, palmtops and different kinds of browsers and document readers.

- The interaction of people and organisations to manage and coordinate the applications, infrastructures and businesses are all necessary to make E-Commerce work.

1.2 E-COMMERCE ACTIVITIES

- E-Commerce activities are playing an important role in our nowadays life and economy.

1.2.1 Various Activities of E-Commerce

- The functions included in E-Commerce are:
  1. Buying and selling of products,
  2. Shipping of products, and
  3. Producing financial statements.
- All this functions are without human interference, which is termed as real 'E' in E-Commerce.
- Humans cannot vanish from the scene . They will be moving to other tasks that generate real value like:
  - Corporate development.
  - Personalised customer service.
  - Sales.
  - New products research etc.
- You will avoid tasks that can be handled faster and more efficiently by a computer such as sending purchase orders, creating journal entries, or confirming shipments etc.
- When a company or oganisation uses computers extensively to perform tasks within the organisations, we call it "E-Commerce ready for capable".
- E-Commerce is a range of online business activities that include explaining products or services are providing a mechanism for customers to buy those products and services from a website or internet and it encompasses online shopping and online purchasing.

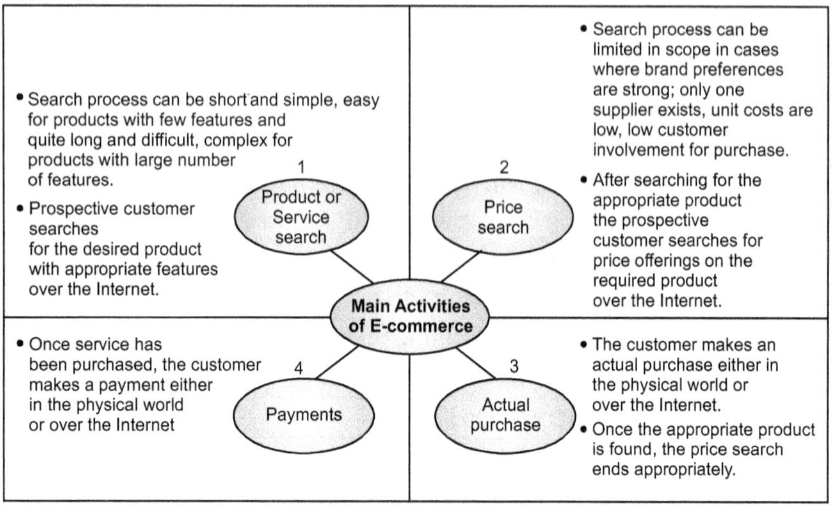

Fig. 1.11: Activities related to a prospective customer in E-Commerce

- Fig. 1.11 shows following major sequential activities of E-Commerce:
  1. **Product or Service Search:** Internet sites offer product feature search and comparison services for relatively complex consumer products that have multiple suppliers. This facilitates the search and evaluation process.
  2. **Price search:** It can be extensive in scope in cases where low or no brand preferences exist, multiple reliable suppliers exist, unit costs are high or the product requires high involvement for purchase. Products and price search can be interactive in some cases.
  3. **Actual purchase:** The sequential activities are in Fig. 1.11 may end at the first or second point without any economic transaction being effected. When the actual purchaser utilises the internet, the economic transaction will be part of electronic commerce.
  4. **Payments:** Once product has been purchased the customers makes the payment either physical or internet world.
- E-Commerce firms/organisations act directly/indirectly in several ways as under, to effect and influence one or more of the four major sequential activities by the prospective customer. The Table 1.1 gives E-Commerce activities.

Table 1.1: Electronic Commerce Activities

1. Direct selling of goods and/or services over the Internet:	This activity involves providing product information, price details on the Internet to enable a customer to buy a product through off-line or online payment mechanisms.
2. Provision of company information on a company homepage:	Though not E-Commerce, provides important information about the company's products and provokes direct or indirect enquiries and subsequent purchase.
3. Priced information:	Firms or organisations may provide priced information regarding products or provide comparative information that may be of value to niche customer. In some cases, the information may be provided free to end-customers as the featured firms/products pay for the service.
4. Advertising banners on popular internet sites for publicity and marketing:	Communicates packaged information regarding the company advertised and provides links to the company's homepage. The host company also earns some revenue by providing advertising space.
5. Research and Development:	Firms or organisations may gather product preference and use information through popular general sites like double click.com through information or through contents and use the information to provide targeted products.
6. Agent services:	Firms or oragnisations may act as internet based agents and provide an internet site that helps in bringing the buyer and seller together and thereby earn commission income.

1.2.2 Various Modes of Operation associated with E-Commerce

- There are Four major modes in E-Commerce:

1. Revenue Generating Modes:

- Firms can develop new revenue generating modes through the appropriate use of internet capabilities. E-Commerce revenue models are used to generate income online and include product and information sales, affiliate marketing, online advertising, subscription services, and transaction fees. Some companies also use subscription services and transaction fees to generate income, such as eBay and Netflix respectively.
- The Revenue Generating Modes adopted are:
  - **Profit from purchase/sale of goods:** Through the reach of the internet in the physical world, trading profits can improve its quantum.
  - **Income from agents:** Agent generates income by bringing the buyer and the seller closely. This is usually charged from the seller. In some cases both parties are charged.
  - **Income from Priced Packaged Information:** Revenue generated from the sale of information that is renedered more valuable to the consumer as it is appropriately collected, classified and in easily searchable form. Through internet capabilities, it can provide greater currency to the information.
  - **Revenues from the Advertisement:** These are the revenues generated through advertisements put as images or scroll bars or pop-ups on popular internet sites. It may be calculated based on "Page –views" or "click throughs".
  - **Income from Priced information:** Priced information regarding products or services are provided to customer. This generates income.
  - **Income from sale of aggregated marketing information:** Firms may like to sell aggregated traffic and customer data to marketing research firms. This is a revenue source for firms.

2. Product Delivery Modes:

- Two types of product delivery modes in electronic commerce are:

  (a) Physical Delivery Mode: In this mode, the delivery through physical shops or through delivery service providers such as courier services. The transaction ends with safe delivery except in cases where the physical product requires maintenance, repairs, replacements and other types of follow-up activity.

In the latter cases, the follow-up can be provided either by local agents of the firm or by the firm itself. Such follow-up can be either through visits or email or a combination of the two.

(b) Virtual Delivery Mode: Typically used for information products (software , reports, music, etc).

The product may be made available for viewing on the screen or for direct download or through e-mail delivery only after payments have been made. Usually through email any follow-up is required.

3. Payment Collection Modes:

- Two types of payment collection modes in electronic commerce are:

  (a) Physical: Payments collected through agents from physical shops or against delivery through delivery services providers such as courier services.

  (b) Virtual: Payments collected through smart cards ,credit cards, charge cards, , gift cheques or e-cash.

4. Operating Modes:

- There can be three major modes of handling electronic commerce business operations:

  (a) Completely outsourced operations: Activities like web-hosting, back-end processing and order fulfillment are outsourced to other specialized firms or a consortia. The firm that builds the product chooses to concentrate on its physical world operations or on manufacturing alone.

  (b) Completely self-handled operations: All E-Commerce related activities like web-hosting, back-end processing and order fulfilment activities are handled by the firm in parallel with its physical world operations and manufacturing.

  (c) Hybrid operations: Part of the E-Commerce activities (typically back-end processing and order fulfilment) are handled by the firm in parallel with its physical world operations and manufacturing. The rest (typically web-hosting) is outsourced to specialised firms.

1.2.3 Elements and Resources impacting E-Commerce and Changes

- E-Commerce has the ability to affect the way that an organization operates in a multidimensional way. Most business strategies have a combinations of the factors such as network practices, cultural change, technology, cost and time frame, management work process consultants, integrators, vendors.

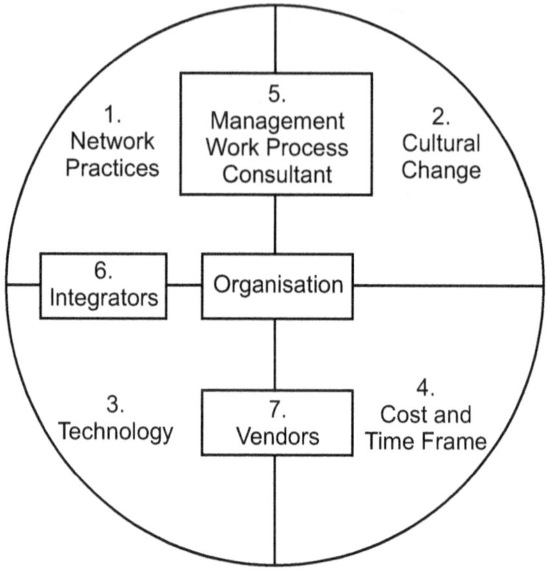

Fig. 1.12: Elements and Resources impacting E-Commerce and Changes

- These elements have direct impact on the development of E-Commerce strategy. So it is important to understand the relationship of these elements to each other.
  - **(a) Network Practices:** This ensures that the program will be supported by new defined and documented methods of working.
  - **(b) Cultural change:** Many E-Commerce systems need significant changes in the way that an organization does business.
  - **(c) Technology:** This provides the infrastructure and components for E-Commerce systems. These are to be developed and deployed to meet the new business, work process and quality goods of the organization.
  - **(d) Cost and time frame:** These are important factors in the development of strategy and the supporting plan. Without a project plan, progress or success ratios for the program cannot be measured.
  - **(e) Management Work Progress consultant:** These services provide with the road map and guide you through the development planning and work process changes critical for the success of the system.

(f) **Integrators:** Professional services companies will provide you with technology advice and development services.

(g) **Vendors:** These are suppliers of technology or Internet E-Commerce services.

1.2.4 Types of E-Commerce Providers and Vendors

(a) E-Commerce Vendor:

- E-Commerce vendors are needed to supply the software and services used to start and operate most online stores. However, they are more significantly known for supplying consumable and durable goods to online shop owners so that they can resell the items at a profit.
- Reliable E-Commerce vendors have quality control systems in place to ensure that purchased products are delivered without damage.

Types of Vendors:

1. Drop Shipping Suppliers:

- These vendors allow retailers to take orders from customers over their websites, and the vendors deliver the products directly to the purchaser.
- Drop shipping is the digital version of being able to "buy low and sell high" with minimal effort. You partner with suppliers that sell you an item at wholesale prices and you sell them to the buyer for the retail price.
- For example: If you want to sell noise-canceling headphones, the supplier cost is ₹1500 and you sell them online for ₹2000. With each sale, you make ₹500 profit.

2. Wholesaler:

- The wholesaler is another type of E-Commerce vendor. Online store owners can purchase items from wholesalers that are below least prices and resell them to their online customers for a profit.

3. Manufacturers of the goods

- Online retail business owners who sell specialty goods often find that the best E-Commerce vendors are the manufacturers of the goods. These e-shop owners can establish purchase agreements with manufacturers, and the results are lower prices and potentially higher profits from sales.

(b) E-Commerce Provider:

- For many manufacturers and wholesale distributors, selecting an E-Commerce provider is a top priority.
- E-Commerce service providers are businesses that provide any combination of consulting, software and computer systems for

E-Commerce Websites (e.g. Internet connection. E-Commerce site hosting, shopping cart integration, payment processing integration etc.

- These service providers are low-cost and also offer free or low cost E-Commerce software for building E-Commerce sites.
- E-Commerce service provider is the fastest and easiest solution to start your online business where all that you need is a business name and a list of products to be sold.
- Some service providers charge monthly flat rates based on the number of items in your online catalog, while a few take A percentage of your sales.
- These service providers take care of all the transaction processing, web servers, backups and so forth.
- Some service providers may even setup a merchant account for you, if you don't have one. However, E-Commerce service providers, can be the least flexible option.
- Many service providers provide a limited set of options to set E-Commerce site and some service providers can also impose hidden charges or lack security and reliability. A business can check capabilities of these service providers by first trying them. Some of these services have a 30 day trial period. Yahoo! Merchant Solutions (small business.yahoo.com/E-Commerce/) is example of a famous E-Commerce service provider.

1.2.5 Opportunity development for E-Commerce stages

- The usage of the stages of E-Commerce can help distributors understand how B2B E-Commerce is unfolding and which firms are winning the battle to move online.

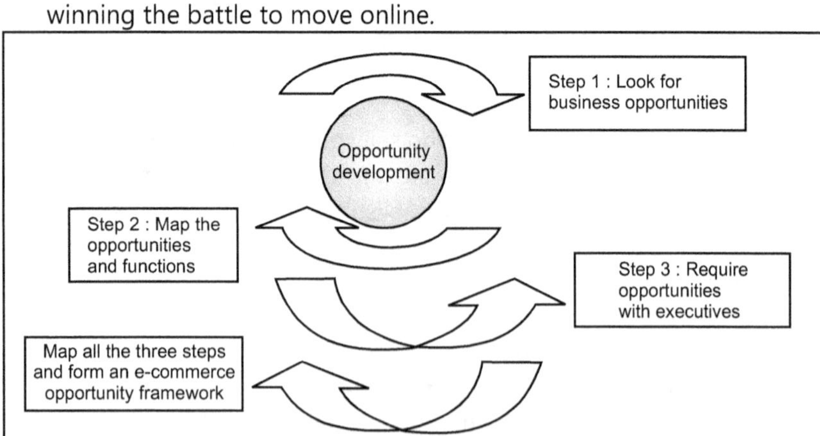

Fig. 1.13: Opportunity Development of E-Commerce Stages

Following steps are included in the Development of E-Commerce business case:

Step 1 : Look for the opportunities which are going to support the primary business goals;
- o Increase sales and client base
- o Shorten the product development time.
- o Reduce inventory
- o Expand the network for partnership.
- o Reduce publishing costs.

Step 2 : Map the opportunities to the individual departments and functions in the organization.
- o Describe how E-Commerce would help.
- o Gain confidence/agreement with department members.
- o Rate the opportunity against the business goals.

Step 3 : Review the opportunities with executives.
- o Begin to quantify the process.
- o Illustrate the opportunities and relevance to the business.

- Map all the three steps together in an E-Commerce opportunity framework.

1.2.6 Development of E-Commerce Business Case

- The business case is a necessary step to build effective solutions. E-Commerce applications often provide very high Return on Investment (ROI).
- The concept of E-Commerce is such that the benefits for businesses are reflected as benefits for consumers.
- **Access to new markets:** Businesses of all sizes can address customers located worldwide without requiring the existence of the local branch.
- **Increase sales:** Companies expand their turnover traders at all latitudes and with minimum operating costs.
- **Increasing competitiveness:** Companies which face competition in their local market extend their business on the Web.
- **Reduction of links in the supply chain:** The supplier is addressed directly to the customer without involving intermediaries.
- **Direct costs Restriction:** Use of ICT for the publication and transmission of information can reduce costs compared with communication and publication in printed form. This is achieved by

reducing the cost of a series of processes involved in a business, such as operating costs, promotion-advertising costs, communication costs with suppliers and consumers, and the cost of production and distribution of goods, especially products transferred electronically.

- **Continuous operation:** Using the Internet allows purchases at any time (24 hours) without any additional financial burden for business.
- **Better communication policy and promotion:** Online transactions allow the mutual relationship between company and consumer. In this way businesses through electronic transactions can gather information on the habits, needs and preferences of consumers and in accordance with them to adapt their policy and to exploit the potential of the Internet offers, management and consumer information.
- **Optimal management of products and orders:** Electronic commerce allows to shorten the time required for the production and delivery of information and services. At the same time, electronic communications accelerate the completion of the transactions, thus increasing the flexibility of business supplies. Businesses utilize this possibility by applying the system JIT (Just-In-Time), which reduces the potential for restocking, thus greatly reducing the cost of production-distribution of their products.
- **Improved company image:** Through faster processing, the transactions with consumers, as well as communication with other businesses, businesses are allowed to improve competitiveness approaching more to the needs of the customer.

1.2.7 Components and factors for the development of the Business Case

- Following factors/components are needed for the development of the business case:

1. Impact on The Organization:

- The most important and difficult part is to decide how your organization is equipped to use E-Commerce technology. This is due to the multifaceted nature of E-Commerce and the various alternatives presents.
- The variables in this issue involved are:
  - o Desire for change
  - o Risk aversion
  - o State of the current operation
  - o Competition and financial stability.

2. Cost Analysis:

- Following points are measured in the process:
  - Tasks in the current environment
  - Comparing these with the expenses after the system has been put in the place.

Estimating the Costs:

- For a good estimate, start with following factors:
  - Identification of the components.
  - Evaluate the incremental staff resources.
  - Try and use existing systems to keep maintenance cost down.
  - Speed up startup time frames.
  - Estimate the cost of technology infrastructure which supports your applications.
  - Calculate ROI.

Cost Estimating Components:

- **Hardware:** Network, routers, servers, desktop, gateways.
- **Software:** Desktop, network, servers, one-time purchases, development costs.
- **Development and implementation:** Training and testing costs ,One-time consulting database population, conversion.
- **Support (maintenance):** Hosting services, Annual system administration, support and maintenance costs.

3. Savings:

- It is better to reuse the existing infrastructure and systems that are already in use. You might be already having standards in place for web servers, databases, browsers and application development tools.
- With these tools, the adoption and maintenance costs of the system will be reduced.

4. The Technology Plan:

- Some technology plan should be worked out and included in the business plan. It should reflect the components that are part of the solution.

5. Network Practices/ Business Processes:

- You may have simple work process requirements such as defining site and product pricing updates. E-Commerce will provide you with the opportunity to improve and cement business partnerships, develop new relationships by offering improved service and support.
- A **business process** is an activity or set of activities that can accomplish a specific organizational goal. Business processes are designed to provide information directly to the person who needs it without intervention.

1.2.8 Steps to Design and Develop an E-Commerce Website

- Website is a set of related web pages containing content such as text, images, video, audio, etc.
- A website is hosted on at least one web server, accessible via a network such as the internet or a Private Local Area Network (PLAN) through an internet address known as a Uniform Resource Locator (URL). All publicly accessible websites collectively constitute the World Wide Web (WWW).
- The process of an E-Commerce website development project has following 7 major steps:

Step 1: Idenfify the product/service, and the customer:

(a) Keep the following points in mind in order to identify the Product/Service:

- It's a crowded market, so target single customer or group of customers.
- Consider the price of the product. Items that are priced very low will make it difficult for you to get returns, but also it is difficult for people to purchase high-value items without seeing them first.
- Availability of the product and convenience can help a customer decide whether to shop online or offline. Items that are usually not available too easily in stores tend to rack up more sales online.
- Do consider the incidental costs. Perishables, fragile goods, voluminous or large goods all pose shipping challenges and drive up costs.
- It is important to be driven about your products and do your best to sell them.

(b) Know your E-Commerce Customer:

- It's vital for any business to understand who their customer is so they can reach out to him/her in the best way possible.
- Keep in mind following parameters to know your customer.
- Establish the demographic i.e. gender, age group, income level, education etc.

- Open social media to identify the people showing interest in your brand/offering through 'likes' and 'follows'
- Interact with customers through feedback, suggestions and reviews to understand the customer profile better.

Step 2: Choose the right E-Commerce website development platform:

- An E-Commerce platform is a software suite that helps you build your E-Commerce store where you make your products available, and where your customers can conduct transactions.
- Choosing the right E-Commerce platform is very important to any online business as it is the foundation of the business.
- To begin with, as the business owner you need to decide whether you'd prefer a self-hosted platform, or a hosted one. While the requirement for both is different, hosted platforms are usually preferred as they usually consist of full-features websites and maintenance plans. This minimizes the scope for error and makes website management much easier.
- Even then, there are many platforms to choose from, the most popular include Hybris, Magento, WooCommerce, or Shopify.
- When choosing your E-Commerce platform, you need to keep your business requirements as well as the features on offer in mind.
- To help you get going, here's list of things to consider:

Database compatibility and integration:

- It's important to ascertain the compatibility of the platform with your existing systems and the ability to integrate them.
- You will probably need professionals to assist you in this, but it is well worth the money and time spent to create a stable online store.
- Scope for E-Commerce website customization: Moreover, each business has different requirements, and it's important for the platform to support these.
- One of our clients had a unique requirement—as a seller of books, they had to accept by their country's laws which allowed them to sell certain books only to people over a specified age.

This made it difficult to sell the books online, but the client needed the book to be listed in the online catalogue to make website visitors aware of its availability.

- To suit this unique case, the project developers were able to create an additional restricted catalog on the E-Commerce website, where visitors could view the listing, but not purchase the books.
- Similarly, grocery E-Commerce websites require the capability to list product or size variants, list perishables with unique weight or size measurements, offer features such a shopping lists. Choosing a platform with good scope for customization makes it possible to enable the development of such features and deliver a good customer user experience.

Payment gateway integration:

- One of the challenges faced by E-Commerce businesses in India is the discomfort with online payments. So it is vital include traditional payment options, such as cash on delivery, along with regular payment options, such as credit and debit card payments and netbanking. It has now also become necessary to provide the option of linking to payment wallets.
- Your E-Commerce platform of choice must support these capabilities.
- If you seek international expansion, then it is important to incorporate multiple currency options to make easy payment for overseas customers.

Strong backend:

- A good online commerce webstore is supported by a strong backend for an organized and easy-to-use admin experience. A high quality platform will provide several admin features such as multiple admin logins, easy changes in inventory, taking stock of orders, and so on.

Mobile-friendly, or responsive E-Commerce:

- Responsive E-Commerce websites, suitable for viewing on mobile phones, are a great alternative. The platform must support a website that is optimized for a mobile-friendly. The easy accessibility leads to increasing amounts of time spent browsing on the phone, which often leads more online as well as in-store purchases.

E-Commerce marketing:

- Do consider the marketing tools offered by the E-Commerce platform—some platforms offer integration with analytics tools, social media websites, promotion tools, etc. Once you go live with the webstore, marketing will form a significant path of business growth, so look forward to the needs for these capabilities and choose your platform accordingly.

Step 3: Choose the right E-Commerce website hosting platform: Choice of server and hosting determines your website's accessibility and performance efficiency. It's very important to choose quality over costs saving when it comes website hosting and support. The key parameters are:

- **Speed:** Your server should have the capacity to deliver good website speed. This is also dependent on the internet connection speed for your server. Providing good speed is vital as not only do customers have little patience for websites that load slowly, but search engines also rank slow-loading websites poorly.
- **Uptime:** A good way to review the kind of service you will get from the host is to check recent uptime records of other websites being hosted by the provider. One of the greatest attributes of E-Commerce is any time, any place availability and shopping convenience. This is enabled by maximizing uptime.
- **Support:** Check for support services that your host provide. Some just provide the infrastructure, while some also give managed services that help minimize troubleshooting response time and improve uptime. Sometimes managed services also cover issue management and upgrades.
- **Scalability:** Choose servers that can adapt to your business needs. This means your website doesn't go down due to an overload in traffic (as the servers scale up to accommodate increased traffic during peak season or offers), as well and optimizes the costs.

- **Security:** As an E-Commerce website, you accept payments online so the servers must be PCI-DSS compliant. It is also important to ensure data security through secure servers.

Step 4: Choose the right E-Commerce development partner: Look out for these following aspects to choose right E-Commerce development company:

- **Location:** Contrary to the popular practice of outsourcing to cheaper locations, it makes plenty of sense to commission E-Commerce website development to a local company. With an intensive task like this, that requires regular and deep involvement, it helps to be in located in the same time zone in order to speed up communication and coordination.
- **Custom development:** Each business has unique needs and circumstances and your E-Commerce website and development process must be adapted to suit these needs. A vendor who takes the time to understand your goals, requirements and hurdles, and takes the time to address them is suitable to deliver a website that will be more to your expectations and will fuel business growth.
- **Approach to processes:** E-Commerce website development is a lengthy and task-intensive project, with goals and hurdles that change along the way. Therefore it is very important to partner with a vendor who follows agile processes that are continuously adapted and improved on the journey to suit the changing needs. Due constancy for quality assurance in processes also helps deliver predictable outcomes and more bang for your buck.
- **Scalability:** Choosing an established E-Commerce website development partner makes resources available as per need without much delay. This ability to scale up or down as per project needs facilitates smooth development and minimizes the time lost to logistic problems.

Step 5: E-Commerce website testing: The next essential step is E-Commerce website testing. Testing checks usability, customer convenience, checks for bugs, and is vital to ensuring a good shopping experience. Testing is usually carried out in various browsers, across platforms, and across devices. Website testing can be manual, or automated, or a combination of the two.

- The importance of testing cannot be stressed enough—slow-loading websites, poor navigation, broken links and bugs have been known to cause losses for E-Commerce websites as customers leave dissatisfied.

  So what is usually checked in the E-Commerce website testing process?
- **The visitor/customer flow:** Each step and page usually taken by the customer on his/her visit is tested, starting from home page to menu, search bar and results, product listing up to payment and checkout, and acknowledgement.
- **The functionalities:** the pages, the categories, filters, user registration, shopping cart, payment options, shipping options—all features and functions offered are checked for usability.
- **Security:** E-Commerce website security is vital, not just on the payments page, where customers share sensitive information like card details and address, but also throughout the rest of the website.
- **Compatibility:** With different browsers, on various platforms, and across devices, as mobile phones and tablets are no longer devices to be ignored when it comes to online shopping.
- **Performance and discoverability:** To ensure the website load time isn't too long, catch broken links, check for SEO ranking in search engines.

Step 6: Adapt and grow:

- It's necessary to continuously adapt to changing conditions and stay ahead of competition.
- Upgrade your platform regularly to keep your website running smoothly and offer up-to-date features. Periodically check for security updates and implement them.
- Track customer browsing habits, purchase patterns, cart abandonment, and other user behavior to tweak your offerings and presentation accordingly.

SUMMARY

- The sharing of business information, maintaining business relations and conducting business transactions by using telecommunication networks is defined as E-Commerce.
- E-Commerce is normally categorized as Business to Business (B2B), Business to Customer (B2C) and Customer to Customer (C2C).
- Development of E-Commerce requires a good computing and communication infrastructure in a country.
- Role of internet and web in E-Commerce are selling products, advertisements, marketing, review, training, communication and data access.
- Technologies used in E-Commerce are EDI, barcodes, e-mails, internet, web, product data exchange, electronic forms.
- Various activities of E-Commerce are online shopping, online ticketing, electronic payments, internet banking and virtual auctions.
- Modes of E-Commerce are revenue generating modes, product delivery modes, payment collection modes, operating modes.
- Elements and resources impacting E-Commerce are network practices, cultural changes, technologies, cost and time frame, management work progress consultant, integrators, and vendors.
- E-Commerce vendors are needed to supply the software and services used to start and operate most online stores.
- E-Commerce service provider is an organization that provides any combination of consulting, software and computer systems for E-Commerce websites.
- The usage of the Stages of E-Commerce can help distributors understand how B2B E-Commerce is unfolding and which firms are winning the battle to move online.
- Essential stages of E-Commerce development which are certainly required for any successful E-Commerce website: Research and Strategy, Preparation of Website Outline, Information Framework, Website Designing, Construction, Migration and Launching.

CHECK YOUR UNDERSTANDING

1. Which of the following describes E-Commerce?
   (a) Doing business (b) Doing business electronically
   (c) Selling goods (d) None of the above
2. Which is the following not a major type of E-Commerce?
   (a) B2B (b) C2A
   (c) C2B (d) C2C

3. Which is the mode of E-Commerce?
   (a) Revenue generating mode
   (b) Product delivery mode
   (c) Operating mode
   (d) All of the above
4. Which is the first step in E-Commerce website design?
   (a) Effective marketing
   (b) Identify the product/service, and the customer
   (c) Testing
   (d) Select E-Commerce website platform
5. ______ is basically a concept of online marketing and distributing of products and services over the internet.
   (a) B2G (b) B2E
   (c) B2C (d) B2B

Answers

1. (b)	2. (c)	3. (d)	4. (b)	5. (c)

PRACTICE QUESTIONS

1. Answers the Following Question in brief:

1. What is E-Commerce?
2. What is B2B E-Commerce?
3. What are C2A and B2A?
4. What is E-mail?
5. What is meant by online shopping?

2. Answer the Following Questions:

1. Define E-Commerce. What are different types of E-Commerce?
2. Explain C2C E-Commerce with an appropriate example.
3. Which are types of E-Commerce vendors?
4. Which are the components and factors for the development of the business case?
5. Write in detail the steps to design and develop an E-Commerce website?

3. **Write short note on:**

   E-Commerce, e-distributor, barcode, e-mail, online ticketing, E-Commerce vendor, E-Commerce e-service provider, business process, pay-per-click, content marketing.

4. **Answer True or False:**

   1. Doing business online is known as E-commerce.
   2. Lack of system security is the disadvantage of E-commerce.
   3. C2C E-commerce is E-commerce between two businesses.
   4. Wholesaler is a type of E-commerce vendor.
   5. Testing is the first step in website design.

Answers

1. (T)	2. (T)	3. (F)	4. (T)	5. (T)

■■■

Unit **2**...

Introduction to E-Marketing

Objectives ...

- Understand the difference between Traditional Marketing and e-Marketing.
- Identify Web Presence Goals.
- Understand E-customer Relationship Management.
- Know about Supply Chain Management.

2.1 E-MARKETING

- E-Marketing is also known as Internet marketing, web-marketing or even online marketing. It is actually a subset of digital marketing.
- E-marketing is the process of marketing a product or service using the Internet. E-Marketing not only includes marketing on the Internet, but also includes marketing done via e-mail and wireless media. It uses a range of technologies to connect businesses to their customers.
- E-mail lists, banner ads, PPC (pay per click), and social media marketing are examples of methods used in Internet marketing.

Types of E-marketing:

- There are several ways in which companies can use internet for marketing. Some ways of E-Marketing are:
  1. **Article marketing:** Article marketing is a branch of content marketing. It is a type of advertising in which companies write and distribute short articles to a range of outlets such as article banks, forums, and newsletter publishers.
  2. **Affiliate marketing:** Affiliate marketing is the process by which an affiliate earns a commission for marketing another person's or company's products.
  3. **Video marketing:** Video marketing is a forward-facing marketing strategy that integrates engaging video into your marketing campaigns.
  4. **Email marketing:** Email marketing is the act of sending a commercial message, typically to a group of people using e-mail.

5. **Blogging:** This is a website containing a writer's or group of writers' own experiences, observations, opinions, etc., and often having images and links to other websites.
6. **Content marketing:** A type of marketing that involves the creation and sharing of online material (such as videos, blogs, and social media posts) that does not explicitly promote a brand but is intended to stimulate interest in its products or services.

Advantages of E-Marketing:

- Certain advantages of E-Marketing are discussed as below:
  1. Internet provides 24 hours and 7 days "24/7" service to its users. So you can build and make customers relationships worldwide, and at any time your customer can shop or order product.
  2. The cost of spreading your message on internet is nothing. Many social media sites like Facebook, Linkedin and Google plus allow you freely advertise and promote your business.
  3. You can easy and instantly update your registered customers or subscribers through e-mail.
  4. Visitors or potential customers of your website can get up to the minute information on each visit.
  5. If you are having a sale, your customers can start shopping at the discounted prices literally as soon as they open their e-mail.
  6. If a company has an information sensitive business, like a law firm, newspaper or online magazine that company can also deliver its products directly to customers without having to use a courier.

2.1.1 Traditional Marketing

- Traditional marketing is a form of conventional marketing that was used before the internet era was widespread.
- It is a convenient mode of marketing that is used for targeting the audience with various offline advertising and promotional methods.
- Most traditional marketing strategies fall under following categories:
  1. Print (magazines, newspapers, etc.)
  2. Broadcast (TV, radio, etc.)
  3. Direct Mail (catalogs, postcards, etc.)
  4. Telephone (telemarketing, SMS marketing, etc.)
  5. Outdoor (billboards, flyers, etc.)

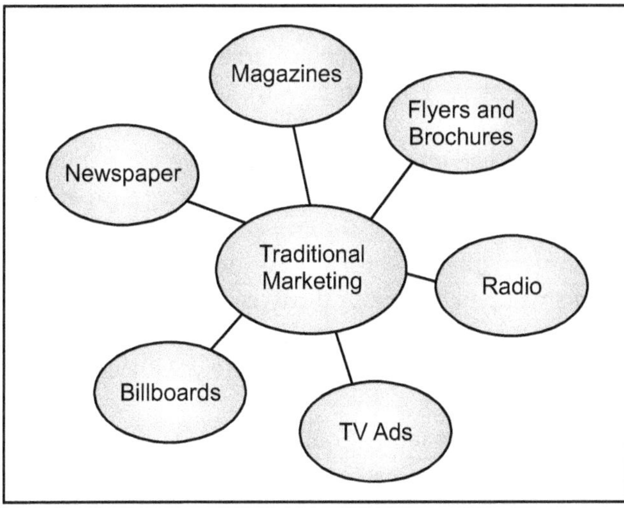

Fig. 2.1: Traditional Marketing Strategies

Who uses Traditional Marketing?

- Nearly every company selling a product or service uses one or more types of traditional marketing as part of an overall advertising strategy.
- Mid-sized companies and large corporations are most likely to use TV commercials. Advertising on television is usually the most expensive form of marketing, with prices depending on the time slots and programming content.
- Entrepreneurs and small businesses, who may have limited marketing budgets, most often use print marketing in newspapers or newsletters to advertise to local customers. Many also place local radio advertisements. Some use direct mail, and a few may employ limited telemarketing.
- While network television commercials are usually out of the budget range for smaller companies, local cable programming has made television advertising more accessible for these types of businesses.

Drawbacks of Traditional Marketing:

- Some of the drawbacks of traditional marketing are:
    - Print can be difficult to measure. Printed advertisements reach different classes of people, who might or might not have an interest in the product. Just because people subscribe to a newspaper or magazine doesn't mean they actually read it.

- Broadcast messages have a shorter lifespan compared with printed messages. Additionally, marketing through television and radio is costlier, compared with other forms of traditional marketing.
- Direct mail marketing can be expensive as a business incurs design and printing costs as well as postage expenses to reach its target.
- Telephone marketing may be inexpensive, but just try getting even a small percentage of those cell phone owners to answer a call from a number they don't recognize. And the number of landlines has dropped commensurately with the growth of cell phones.

2.1.2 Identifying Web Presence Goals

- **Web presence:** A Web presence (or Web site) is a collection of Web files on a particular subject that includes a beginning file called a home page .
- For example, most companies, organizations, or individuals that have Web sites have a single address that they give you. This is their home page address.
- From the home page, you can get all the other pages on their site. For example, the Web site for PRAGATI has the home page address http://www.pragati.com.
- One method of measuring your **web presence** is by counting the number of customers who have visited your website within a given period of time.

Web Presence Goals:

- A firm's physical location rarely is image-driven. Physical location must satisfy many other business goals unrelated to image and presence
- On the web, businesses have the luxury of intentionally creating a space that creates a distinctive presence.
- The web site can perform many image-enhancing tasks very effectively, including:
  - Serving as a sales brochure.
  - Serving as a product showroom.
  - Showing a financial report.
  - Posting an employment ad.
  - Serving as a customer contact point.
- Businesses must decide which tasks their website must accomplish and which tasks are the most important to include.

2.1.3 Achieving Web Presence Goals

- An effective web site is the one that creates an attractive presence that meets the objectives of the business or the organization.
- Some methods to meet the objectives include the following:
  - Provide detailed but useful facts/information to establish a sense of the company's presence.
  - Provide list of services offered.
  - Provide search/help features.
  - Use links to get the visitor to explore points of interest, keep them on site, and encourage return visits.
  - Provide information that is relevant to the customer's needs.
  - Use colorful and interesting images to enhance the appearance of the site; provide the visitor the option to select thumbnails to reduce download time.
  - Allow the visitor the option to select a Flash or non-Flash version of the site in order to reduce file size and download time.
  - Provide the customer with a connection-type option for streaming audio/video clips.
  - Keep the site user-friendly: allow visitors to "experience the site in different ways and at different levels".
  - Build flexibility into the site's interface to meet the needs of a wide range of visitors.
  - Provide information about products and how to use them.
  - Provide a "two-way contact channel" between visitors and the company.
  - Provide security for transmission of personal information.

2.1.4 Uniqueness of the Web

- Here are some of the uniqueness that you can add in your Ecommerce website while creating one:
  - **Ease of Use:** Online sellers have only a minimum amount of time to make a sale. So focus on the user experience by providing shopping filters, categories and comparison capabilities.
  - **Wish Lists:** Wish-lists helps the customer to add their interested product form Ecommerce website to wish list and make a purchase now or later.

- **Find-in-Store:** Not every customer can find their need product in your home page. So, it is must to have a find-in-store option. This makes it incredibly helpful to see which local stores have products in stock.
- **Related Items:** Providing Related Item option in your Ecommerce website will let the customer find a similar product to their search result. This will make the customer to check out the related item and if they like the product, it will lead to a successful purchase
- **Frequently Asked Questions (FAQ):** Before purchasing a product customer will definitely like to know about the product. So, providing an FAQ section will help the consumer to get every related question from FAQ site in your Ecommerce website.
- **Social Proof:** Social media is the next big thing to make your website more famous. Linking Social profile in your Ecommerce website is one of the must-have features that help to increase your brand character.
- **Security Features:** Online transactions have become an integral part of our lives. Meanwhile, Ecommerce website can be a target for cyber criminals. So it is mandatory for an Ecommerce website to provide high-security features.
- **Advanced Payment Options:** Providing an advanced payment options. Customers will do a regular purchase only if they are satisfied with the payment gateway.
- **Shipping Information:** When a purchase is made successfully, it should be shipped for delivery. Most of the shopping cart neglect unexpected shipping cost. So provide proper information about shipping while making a purchase.
- **Return Policy:** It is essential for an Ecommerce website to include Return Policy feature. It is one of the trust building factors of online selling. It gives an assurance and builds trust towards your website to the customers.

2.1.5 Meeting the Needs of Website Visitors

- Businesses that are successful on the Web realize that every visitor to their website is a potential customer. Thus, an important concern for businesses crafting a Web presence is the variation in the visitors' characteristics. Visitors visit a website for a specific reason.

- The Web designer who makes a site useful for everyone, needs to keep in mind some of the possible reasons listed as follows:
  - Learning about products or services that the company offers.
  - Buying the products or services that the company offers.
  - Obtaining information about warranties or service and repair policies for products they have purchased.
  - Obtaining general information about the company or organization.
  - Obtaining financial information for making an investment or credit-granting decision.
  - Identifying the people who manage the company or organization.
  - Obtaining contact information of a person or a department in the organization.

2.1.6 Site Adhesion: Content, Format and Access

Content:

- A customer accesses a website for the content of that site. Initially a customer will want to navigate quickly to gain a clear understanding of the site's progression to more detailed information. The key to this is to match a user's psychological and technological sophistication profile with that of the site's initial and subsequent impact.
- Web content refers to the textual, aural or visual content published on a website. Content means any creative element, for example, text, applications, images, archived e-mail messages, data, e-services, audio and video files, and so on.
- Web content is the key behind traffic generation to websites. Creating engaging content and organizing it into various categories for easy navigation is most important for a successful website. Also, it is important to optimize the web content for search engines so that it responds to the keywords used for searching.

Format:

- The format of an organization's site is important with respect to the customer's technical sophistication. Vendors need to crate a balance between information provision and information delivery speed. The selection of data format is crucial, as initially the goal is to create viewer interest and engage the viewer in a prolonged interaction.

- An effective website must convey content to its readers through attractive formatting. Poor formatting can make a website unappealing or even unreadable.
- With Hypertext Markup Language (HTML), you can control a website's formatting so that it appears exactly as you wish. Furthermore, Cascading Style Sheets (CSS) allow you the ability to format a website using an external style sheet. This technique is useful if you wish to apply the same styling to multiple pages within your site.

Access:

- Online data access depends on the bandwidth requirement. The clear rule in the initial interaction phase is to use a minimal a bandwidth as is feasible to facilitate as wide an audience as possible.

2.1.7 Maintaining a Website

- Owning a website comes with certain responsibilities. You can't just build it and forget it. Regular website maintenance is a must if you want your site to be successful.
- Regular maintenance tasks are:
    1. **Keep your site secure:** Websites get hacked, and hacked sites lose visitors and traffic. Setting up a regular monitoring service will ensure that if you do get infected or have site errors, you can fix them fast.
    2. **Keep a regular backup schedule:** Backing up your site should be done regularly, especially for those who update their site often. If the server crashes for some reason, or your site gets hacked, or you make some major mistake, your edits could be gone.
    3. **Keep updated Software:** Most websites are built on a content management system, which means its software can potentially be broken. Third party software, like your ecommerce software, WordPress and Joomla for example, are always updating their software. You need to keep on top these updates and install them as soon as they come out. The updates won't just be new features, they will include security updates too.
    4. **Check the broken links:** Prevent disgruntled users because something doesn't work or you provided a broken link.
    5. **Keep updated content:** Keep regular visitors happy by giving them fresh, updated information and exciting news.

6. **Test Website Speed:** Testing the download speed of your site regularly is important. Especially if you have added a new feature. Web surfer has a very short attention span. If your site is slow to load, they are not going to wait. You need to do everything you can to improve the download speed of your site or blog so visitors stay to read your content .
7. **Track your site statistics:** Look at your web server stats to determine your website traffic. If your web hosting account doesn't have website stats then get one installed. It provides features such as Pages entered on and left on, Time spent on the site, Bounce rate, Referring sites, Countries your visitors are from, Keywords/phrase that were used to find you.

2.1.8 Metrics Defining Internet Units of Measurement

- The E-Commerce world has, since inception been attempting to measure parameters associated with the Web and Websites in order to access two things:
  1. **Advertising:** How many people saw our banner ad?
  2. **Visitation:** How many people came to our site?
- Nevertheless, there are several broad categories of measurements that should be considered for use in accessing performance of E-Commerce units:
  - traffic and site usage metrics
  - marketing metrics
  - financial metrics
  - other performance metrics
  - multi-dimensional scorecards
- Here we consider only internet units of measurement that is shown by traffic and site usage metrics.

Traffic And site usage metrics

- Site traffic analysis can help determine the volume of traffic on a website, as well as which sections of a website are visited, when they are visited, by whom they are visited and where the visitors came from. Traffic volume can be measured in a variety of ways: hits, page views, ad views or banner impressions, visits, and unique visitors.
- **Hits:** Hit is each download of any information from the website. Information can be a page, a picture or a link.

- **Page views:** Each download of an entire page of information.
  A measure of the number of times a page with a banner ad or other advertisement is viewed during a period of time.
- **Ad views or banner impressions:** A collection of webpages a visitor views in a time period while on a website.

Visits:

- **Unique visitors:** The number of non-repeating visitors in a specific timeframe measures the volume of activity in terms of purported individuals, although it is really computers (i.e., IP addresses) rather than individuals that are counted in this type of analysis (i.e. many individuals may share a single computer or a single IP address).

Site usage metrics:

- Site usage metrics help an e-business assess the effectiveness of is E-Commerce website.
- Site usage can be analyzed spatially or temporally. Spatial usage analysis can identify visitor behaviour according to:
  - **Top entry pages:** Pages most commonly entered.
  - **Top exist pages:** Pages most commonly exited from (exit pages can represent leakage from a website, indicating premature exit by visitors).
  - **Most visited pages:** Pages most frequently visited.
  - **Least visited pages:** Pages least visited.
  - **Single visit pages:** Pages only visited once (they may represent trouble spots in the website).
  - **Paths within site:** Most common paths taken by visitors (these may represent design problems if the most common path does not lead to successful completion of an E-Commerce transaction or other site objective).

2.1.9 Online Marketing

- Online marketing is a method that uses the internet to promote or transmit a message about a company's product and services to the potential buyers or target audience.
- Online marketing is also known as internet marketing, web marketing, digital marketing and search engine marketing (SEM).
- Online marketing can deliver benefits such as:
  - Growth in potential
  - Reduced expenses
  - Elegant communications
  - Better control
  - Improved customer service
  - Competitive advantage

Online Marketing Communication:

- Following are online marketing communication options.

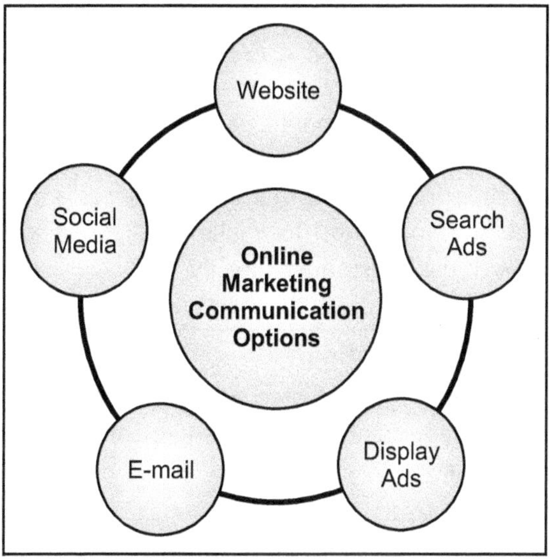

Fig. 2.2: Online Marketing Communication Options

- **Website:** A company must design its website that considers its purpose, products, services, mission and vision. A website should look interesting to view to encourage multiple visits.
- **Search Ads:** Pay-per-click ads is the most important element of the Search Ads. When a visitor searches any term on the search engine, the ad of the marketers appear either on the top of the results or next to it. These appear to identify its significance with respect to the keyword searched. Only when the visitor clicks on the ads, advertisers pay for it.
- **Search Engine Optimization (SEO)** entails the activities that improve the probability that a particular link will appear in the top among all the non-paid links when the visitor searches for a particular keyword.
  - **Display Ads:** Display ads or otherwise called as banner ads are the one that appears in a tiny rectangular box that encompasses text and sometimes graphics, which marketers pay on the placement on specific websites. The cost depends on the traffic on a website, meaning that the more the number of visitors, higher is the cost.

- **E-Mail:** E-mail is quite productive and reasonable selling tools as it enables advertisers to message in order to communicate with a large audience base at a comparatively low cost.
- **Social Media Marketing:** It is one of the emerging modes of marketing these days. Consumers share their videos, audios, texts, and images through various social media platforms Facebook, Twitter, Google plus, Instagram, Linkedin, Pinterest, etc. with their friends, relatives, acquaintances and companies. It facilitates the marketers to make their presence online and connect with their customers directly

2.1.10 Advantages and Disadvantages of Online Marketing

Advantages of Online Marketing:

1. A company can grow faster and reach the target audience through a broader range of marketing elements.
2. It has a competitive advantage over traditional means of marketing.
3. It is easy to trace the number of unique visitors, average session duration, click on an ad, and so forth.
4. Contextual placement is one of the important features of online marketing wherein the marketers can buy ads on the websites which akin to their own products and services.
5. Marketers can also place the ads on the basis of the keywords typed by the customers on Google and other search engines like Bing and Yahoo, to reach the target audience.

Disadvantages of Online Marketing:

1. Fake clicks on the ads done by software-powered websites.
1. Hacking of the website is possible, which results in the loss of control over the messages.
1. Lack of tangibility.

2.2 E-CUSTOMER RELATIONSHIP MANAGEMENT

- Customer Relationship Management (CRM) is a technology for managing all your company's relationships and interactions with customers and potential customers.
- A CRM system helps companies stay connected to customers, streamline processes, and improve profitability.
- Start-ups, large enterprises, and verticals like real-estate, healthcare, insurance, legal, media, restaurants, travel, banking, tax, freelancers,

and non-profits all use a customer relationship management software for increasing their sales, marketing, and customer support efforts.

- Electronic Customer Relationship Management or e-CRM is the process of managing relationships with customers through electronic and information technology. In e-CRM, firms depend highly on the Internet and electronic technology to integrate their internal resources with marketing strategies with a view to fulfilling customers needs.
- Obtaining information in e-CRM is more convenient and intra-organizational collaboration through this system becomes more efficient to communicate with customers. It uses all traditional methods to build and maintain personal relationships with customers, and in addition, it uses the Internet, e-mail, wireless and PDA technologies. Organizations, favoured.

2.2.1 Definition of CRM

- Various authors have defined e-CRM from different view points, but the focus remains on developing a long-term bond with customers through electronic technology. Some of the important definitions are presented here:
  - Parvatiyar and Seth defined e-CRM as an E-enabled comprehensive strategy and process of acquiring, retaining and partnering with selective customers to create superior value for the company and the customer.
  - Laudon and Traver defined as E-CRM an Internet marketing technology, is a repository of customer information that records all of the contacts that a customer has with a firm and generates a customer profile available to everyone in the firm with a need to 'know the customer'.
  - According to P. T. Joseph, e-CRM is the aligning of business strategy with the corporate culture of the organization, along with customer information and a supporting information technology of the customer interactions that promote a mutually beneficial relationship between the customer and the enterprise.
  - The definition given by Strauss et al. is that E-CRM is the application of electronic technology for establishing, maintaining, enhancing and commercializing customer relationship through promise fulfillment.

- The most important definition of e-CRM was given by Chartered Institute of Marketing: E-CRM is making all kinds of interactions between all the parties involved possible not just between firms and customers, but also with intermediaries and other business partners using electronic channels.

2.2.2 Architecture of E-CRM

- Advancement of electronic technology during the recent years has greatly enhanced e-CRM possibilities. The organizational structure of e-CRM has become fully automated and computer mediated. Several e-CRM toolkits have made the process more comprehensive and convenient
- E-CRM architecture facilitates collecting data, warehousing it, analysing it to convert it into a form that can be presented before the users to build and maintain sustainable relationship with customers.
- It enables an organization to establish a one-to-one relationship with its customers and to present a single point of contact to them. Personal interaction with customers is preserved in e-CRM and the information derived from that is used to tailor future interactions.
- Through this seamless communication process, e-CRM allows marketers to derive maximum value from the relationship and also to satisfy customers.
- The basic architecture of e-CRM integrates the front-end marketing activities and processes with the supporting back-end processes. META Group (1999) provided the e-CRM architectural frame work emphasizing three primary components: operational e-CRM, analytical e-CRM and collaborative e-CRM.

2.2.3 Marketing Automation

- Marketing automation is a process where you can save time by handling a number of repetitive tasks and actions automatically based on lead actions and scheduled events.
- **Marketing automation can be thought of like a bridge between your leads and customers:** Marketing automation starts by tracking every lead, or visitor, to your website, or other online locations (in fact, you can even use marketing automation for in-store tracking but that's a different post). This tracking happens similar to Google Analytics tracking just the basic information on each lead, what pages they visit and how long they stay for.

  Here is a list of the key features that you need to look out for in a marketing automation platform.

1. CRM Integration:

- Marketing teams deal with enormous data sets that help them:
  - o Understand the customer journey.
  - o Identify customer requirements based on their behavior and interactions.
  - o Provide a steady stream of marketing-qualified leads to the sales team.
  - o Help curate the right kind of content for customers.
  - o Provide feedback to the operations team regarding product quality.
- An automation software that can pull data from your existing tools such as the Customer Relationship Management (CRM), Customer Data Platform (CDP), Content Management System (CMS), analytics suite, etc. will help streamline your effort and improve the organization's ability to collaborate.
- Integration capabilities should be simple and require minimal staff training. API access to integrate with existing tools, third-party applications, or features that you may need in the future is a bonus.

2. Lead Management:

- Lead management is a fundamental feature of any marketing automation platform. With this feature you should be able to:
  - o Identify prospects and capture leads.
  - o Map their movement across the sales funnel.
  - o Monitor and track potential buyers.
  - o Personalize content and sales outreach.

3. Email Marketing:

- Email marketing is a tried and tested method for customer outreach, and enterprises seek to automate their e-mail campaigns to scale their marketing efforts. The automation platform you choose should have e-mail capabilities such as:
  - o Triggered e-mail – based on events, time, occasions, etc.
  - o Personalized e-mails to create engagement and promote customer retention.
  - o Scheduled messages.
  - o Prioritizing e-mail groups – to sort, categorize, etc.

- Tracking e-mail campaigns to validate and help reduce the bounce rate
- Recording communication and customer behavior by the number of opens, clicks, etc.

4. Social marketing:

- Any marketing automation software should provide social media automation. You should be able to easily integrate your social media with your software so that you can track and analyze customers' social presence and activities. Also, it will allow you to post messages on various social media channels.

5. Campaign Management:

- Campaigns are the workflows you use to nurture leads along the sales cycle. Campaigns have both timed and triggered events. To run successful campaigns you need to send direct and personalized e-mails to a large number of people. Make sure campaign management within your platform supports both inbound marketing and outbound campaigns as well.

6. Visitor Tracking:

- Monitor every person who visits your website by tracking their behaviour, including which pages they click, from where they access the website, what keywords they typed on Google that directed them to your website etc. Many applications deliver real-time alerts to sales representatives when a lead, prospect or customer visits the website. Visitor tracking should also be able to segment your database upon those tracked activities.

7. Landing Pages:

- Also known as a call to action page, a landing page is any page on a website where traffic is sent specifically to prompt a certain action. Landing pages help increase conversion rates through targeted promotion. You can market multiple products to audiences using highly customized landing pages with specifically targeted content.
- The benefits of implementing marketing automation are:
  - **Enhanced marketing processes:** More streamlined and cost-efficient processes, which can be followed by even a novice marketer.
  - **Greater ability to reach to audience:** Hundreds and thousands advertises can be shown using multiple channels, which increases marketing productivity.

- **Effective Closed Loop Marketing (CLM):** Closed loop marketing is a highly effective method of collecting and analyzing customer data from multiple channels. This method use using the information to create targeted content for groups of customers. Marketing Automation ensures effective implementation of CLM.
- **Improved marketing knowledge:** Reporting facility increases marketer's insight into customers, campaigns, market trends, etc.
- **Instant response:** The marketers can respond to an opportunity immediately without being a part of annual campaign plan.
- **Increased customer experience:** Marketing Automation ensures sending no spam mails. On the contrary, it sends the customers only appropriate offers at right times.

2.2.4 Enterprise Customer Management

- An enterprise creates CRM , together with the automation of other aspects of the organization like sales, customer service and back-office functions.
- Information technology plays an important role in collecting, processing and using this customer information in order to attract, retain, and win back customers.
- The management of customer information in companies and organizations is increasingly essential to the maximization of customer value through long term relationships.
- Customer information can be used for different purposes. allowing a company to :
  - reduce overall marketing costs by developing and executing more effective targeted campaigns;
  - increase customer satisfaction and retention by enabling service employees and call center representatives to be more responsive to customers:
  - increase sales by offering products and services that meet the wants and needs of its best customers;
  - improve customer communication by utilizing the customer's preferred communication channels; and finally
  - achieve a higher return on investment by increasing profitability per customer and sale.

2.2.5 Customer Relationship Management Areas

- CRM systems cover many different areas, including sales activities, integrated marketing, and customer support and service. However, a company may choose to use a CRM system for only part of the activities.

- The key business process areas of CRM (Customer Relationship Management) are:
  - **Service:** The CRM has the ability to drive profitability with the support of marketing and sales service. It also drives service revenues.
  - **Sales:** The CRM enables the gain, retain and grow profitable relationship by functioning sales forecasting and planning. It also manages the accounts, activities, billing, contacts, contracts, quotations, pricing, orders and product configuration.
  - **Marketing:** The customer demands and marketing processes are aligned by CRM using some functions to improve. They are the management of marketing analytics, marketing resources, lists, segments, leads, campaigns and trade promotions.
  - **Partner Channel Management:** Managing partner relationship using loyal indirect channel, gaining more profits and giving authority to channel partners can be done by the use of CRM.
  - **Web Channel Enablement:** The Web Channel Enablement maximizes sales and minimizes cost of transaction by the use of the integrated web channel. It increases more profits and also helps to reach new markets. It includes the support of e-commerce, e-marketing, e-service and analytics of the web channel.
  - **Running an Interaction Center:** The customer interaction center maximizes customer cut cost, revenue, and loyalty by transforming into the strategic delivery channel.
  - **Real time Offer Management:** The CRM changes interactions of customers into opportunities for developing relationship and producing revenue. It helps to plan, improve and perform cross selling, up selling and retaining offers and so on.

2.2.6 CRM processes

- The process can be defined as the way in which things are done within an organization. CRM process involves the activities and strategies that companies use to manage their interaction with current and potential customers.
- A simple, step-by-step guide for businesses implementing a CRM process, also called a Customer Relationship Management process.

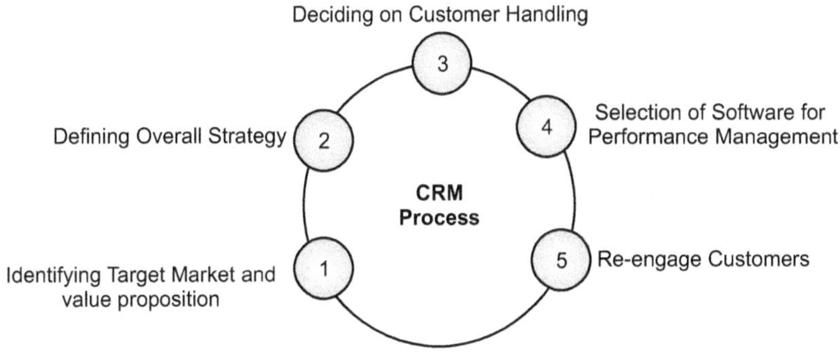

Fig. 2.3: CRM Process

Here is CRM process in 5 simple steps:

Step 1 : Identify Target Market and Value Proposition.

This is the first step in establishing a CRM Process. Most business owners will have this well documented in a business plan.

Different customers may also have different value propositions, but knowing what is important to each type of customer is what sets the CRM process up for success.

Step 2 : Define Overall CRM Strategy and consider Costs.

This is based on what type of customer service and relationship management will work better for your business, and your customers.

Step 3 : Define How Each Customer Type will be Handled.

For example: Consumers are customers which are a lower priority. They will likely only purchase the product once for personal use.

The higher pricing level is for B2B customers. These are developers who use the product to customize, and then resell to their clients. This pricing level is much higher, so these customers receive lifetime dedicated customer support.

Step 4 : Select a CRM Software to Measure Performance.

Every organization will install a CRM SOFTWARE to measure the performance of its strategy. A CRM software helps in reducing the complexity of the process. The best CRM software solutions include SAAS (Software As A Service delivered online), and innovations. This ensures that there is no need of an in-house IT team and server space which would have been expensive.

Step 5 : Re-engage Customers.

Customer engagement is a complex and never-ending task. Customers should be regularly engaged in the organizations products and services. This will help in creating a reminder in the minds of customers.

Customer engagement is a hard task to bring to perfection. Three of the most used forms of customer re-engagement in the CRM Process are: Customer satisfaction surveys, Email, and Social media.

2.2.7 Architectural Components of a CRM solution

- A CRM architecture outlines the strategy, structure, and processes necessary for successful customer relationship management. CRM software plays a central role in implementing this architecture.
- The various components involved in architecture are:

1. **Customer's information repository:**

- It is the database that holds the customer information and serves as the central collective memory of the organization. It continues to collect meaningful information about every customer contact irrespective of the promotions, marketing staff's turnover etc. As long as the information is manageable(identification and availability), it will be adequate and serves as CRM foundation.
- Tools and technologies associated and important to the data repository are: Data extraction tools, Cleansing tools, The relational database used and House holding software.

2. **Campaign Management:**

- Campaign manager occupies the next place to the customer information repository after it is installed. It allows the enterprise to segment the customer base and develop offers. Further, it enables an organization to evaluate the success and flexibility of its marketing programs. It acts as a link between analysis and execution.

3. **Event Triggers/Business Logic and Rules Repository:**

- An event is the trigger condition that initiates a workflow rule.
- Event based marketing (also called trigger marketing and event initiated marketing) is a form of marketing that identifies key events in the customer and business lifecycle. When an event occurs a customer specific marketing activity is undertaken. It has good action rates because it is initiated when a customer is more likely to be active in a decision process.

- Event triggers are an important aspect of:
  - o Direct-mail-oriented database marketing.
  - o Emerging forms. E.g. internet marketing

Business Logic and Rules Repository:

- A business rules management system (BRMS) is used to develop, store, edit, and execute business rules. Business rules are logical statements that define the behavior and operation of a business.
- Business rules consist of a collection of conditions and actions that can be used to enforce simple business logic of an organization. Conditions consist of a field, operator and operand (value, type or expression) that make up a logical statement that evaluates to true or false. If all the conditions of a rule evaluate to true, then the actions are executed.

4. Forecasting and Planning tools:

- Forecasting and Planning tools are the link between an enterprise's front and back offices solving the problem of the two areas being out of synchronization.

  CRM solution provides:
  - o The marketing department with linkage to the back-office environment.
  - o Allows the organization to forecast properly.
  - o Allows to deliver the promises committed to the customers by the marketing and sales people.

2.2.8 Electronic Customer Relationship Management

- **Definition:** Electronic customer relationship management (E-CRM) is the application of Internet-based technologies such as e-mails, websites, chat rooms, forums and other channels to achieve CRM objectives.
- It is a well-structured and coordinated process of CRM that automates the processes in marketing, sales and customer service.

2.2.8.1 Features of E-CRM

- E-CRM software systems may contain a selection of the following features:
  - **(i) Customer Management:** Provides access to all customer information including enquiry status and Correspondence.
  - **(ii) Knowledge Management:** A centralised knowledge base that handles and shares customer Information.

(iii) **Account Management:** Access to customer information and history, allowing sales teams and customer service teams to function efficiently.

( ) **Case Management:** Captures enquiries, escalates priority cases and notifies management of unresolved issues.

( ) **Back-end Integration:** Blends with other systems such as billing, inventory and logistics through relevant customer contact points such as websites and call centres.

( ) **Reporting and Analysis:** Report generation on customer behaviour and business criteria

2.2.8.2 Need and Benefits of E-CRM

- E-CRM provides the ability to capture, integrate, and distribute data gained on the organization's Web site throughout the enterprise. Many organizations are considering adopting the concept of electronic Customer Relationship Management (e-CRM). E-CRM solution supports marketing, sales and service.
- With the advancement of Web-based technology, market dynamics are driving companies to adopt e-CRM.
- The benefits of E-CRM include the following:

1. **Improved customer relations, service and support.**

- CRM provides more avenues for customers to communicate and explain their needs to the organization through numerous contact points. For example, ICICI Bank maintains a list of priority customers and provides them with additional facilities and special offers such as free tickets to concerts, movies, and so on.

2. **Customization of market offerings.**

- Companies can customize a product or service depending on the data available with the firm. The firm can facilitate customer-company interaction through the company contact centre and web site. Such interactions help develop customized products.

3. **Reduction in the customer defection rate.**

- CRM emphasizes on training and development of the employees to become more customer oriented. Due to CRM training and development, employees show care and concern towards the valuable customers; therefore, the customer defection rate may be reduced to a great extent.

4. **Increase and improvement in long-term relationships.**

- Some firms treat their customers as partners. Firms solicit the help of the customers to design new products or to improve their services. If the customer gets involved with the firm, they are more likely to remain with the firm.

5. **Increase in customer equity.**

- CRM increases customer equity. Firms focus the marketing efforts more on the most valuable customers (MVCs). The main aim of CRM is to produce high customer equity. Customer equity is the sum of lifetime values of all customers. More focus on MVCs will enable a firm to increase the customer equity.

6. **Competitive advantage.**

- The firms that adopt CRM get competitive advantage in the market. They can face the competition with much ease. Competitive advantage helps in generating higher returns on investment.

7. **Building and maintaining corporate image.**

- The image of the firm also gets enhanced. Loyal customers become evangelists. The evangelists spread a good word about the company and its products. This enables a firm to get additional customers to its fold.

8. **Higher return on investment.**

- Due to CRM, a company gains a position to generate higher returns on investment. This is because of the repeat purchases on the part of the loyal customers. The company also makes money through cross selling. The higher return on investment increases the shareholders' value.

2.2.8.3 Architecture of E-CRM

- Several E-CRM toolkits have made the process more comprehensive and convenient.
- E-CRM architecture facilitates collecting data, warehousing it, analysing it to convert it into a form that can be presented before the users co build and maintain sustainable relationship with customers.
- It enables an organization to establish a one-to-one relationship with its customers and to present a single point of contact to them. Personal interaction with customers is preserved in e-CRM and the information derived from.

E-CRM architecture would comprise:

- **Sales force automation: Sales force automation** (SFA) is an integrated application of customizable customer relationship management (**CRM**) tools that **automate** and streamline **sales** inventory, leads, forecasting, performance and analysis.
- **E-mail management system:** Email management systems centrally capture e-mails created and received by employees. Using a classification scheme to manage this content, retention periods and access controls can be applied to manage e-mails.

- **Interactive voice response:** CRM integrated IVR solutions allow a business to store customer information, resolve customer service issues, or accomplish routine tasks. By retrieving customer information from the CRM, IVR can play personalised messages and prompts to every approaching customer.
- Knowledge management.
- Call centers.
- Instant online querying through chat.

OR

- The following is a set of technical e-CRM capabilities and applications that collectively and ideally comprise a full e-CRM solution. They are,
    - Customer analytic software.
    - Data mining software.
    - Campaign management software
    - Business simulation software.
    - Real time decision engine.

Customer Analytic Software:

- Customer analytic software predicts, measures, and interprets customer behaviours, allowing companies to understand the effectiveness of E-CRM efforts across both inbound outbound channels. Most importantly, customer analytic should integrate with customer-communications software to enable companies to transform customer findings into ROI-producing initiatives.

Data Mining Software:

- Data mining software builds predictive models to identify customers most likely to perform a particular behaviour such as purchase an upgrade or churn from the company. Modeling must be tightly integrated with campaign management software to keep pace with multiple campaigns running daily or weekly.

Campaign Management Software:

- Campaign management software leverages the data warehouse to plan and execute multiple, highly targeted campaigns overtime, using triggers that respond timed events and customer behaviour. Campaign management software tests various offers against control groups, capture promotion history for each customer and prospect, and produces output for virtually any on-line or off-line customer touch point channel.

Business Simulation:

- Business simulation used in conjunction with campaign management software optirnises offer; messaging and channel delivery prior to the execution of campaigns, and compares planned costs and ROI projections with actual results. **A Real time decision engine** co-ordinates and synchronises communications across disparate customer touch point systems. It contains business intelligence to determine and communicate the most appropriate message, offer, and channel delivery in real time, and support two-way dialogue with the customer.

2.2.8.4 Applications of E-CRM

- The various E-CRM applications can be seen in the following in industry segments:
    - **Banking and finance:** The widespread use of the ATM, credit cards, debit cards, smart cards, and lending through e-CRM via the Internet. This type of computer-based bank-to-bank, bank to consumer and consumer-to-consumer transactional and informational exchange has been referred to as Electronic Commerce (EC).
    - **Benefits:** Relationship with customers, Using e-mail for business communication, Personalized services or one to one services, Website to market products or services, Transaction security.
    - **Hospitality:** The hospitality industry is all about customer interaction. Companies that rely on their guests' comfort and contentment need all of the feedback tools available to make sure they are meeting their customers' needs and expectations.

      E-CRM or Web based CRM E-CRM application in hotel industry are straddling across business functions to retain, capture and capitalize on customer data, i.e. integrating all aspects of business process and systems by keeping the customers as the core.
    - **Telecom:** CRM in the telecom industry can serve as a powerful tool to increase sales and improve customer engagement.
    - **Transport: CRM** software helps benefit business profitability focusing on timely updating customer information and fast order processing. It also allows to organize efficient shipping of FCL/LCL freight and delivery of dangerous/perishable goods.

- **Courier:** The **courier CRM** software helps businesses to provide effective customer service, increase productivity, and drive growth.
- **Government organizations:** Government CRM is a business strategy to provide comprehensive service from all public organizations

2.3 SUPPLY CHAIN MANAGEMENT(SCM)

- Supply Chain Management is the management of the flow of goods and services and includes all processes that transform raw materials into final products. It involves the active streamlining of a business's supply-side activities to maximize customer value and gain a competitive advantage in the marketplace.
- Supply Chain Management can become increasingly important to your organization as global markets and networks expand. Through supply chain management, you can boost customer service, reduce operating costs and improve your company's financial position. Supply chain management can also have a larger global impact, such as reducing pollution and energy consumption and assisting in distribution of goods in a disaster situation.

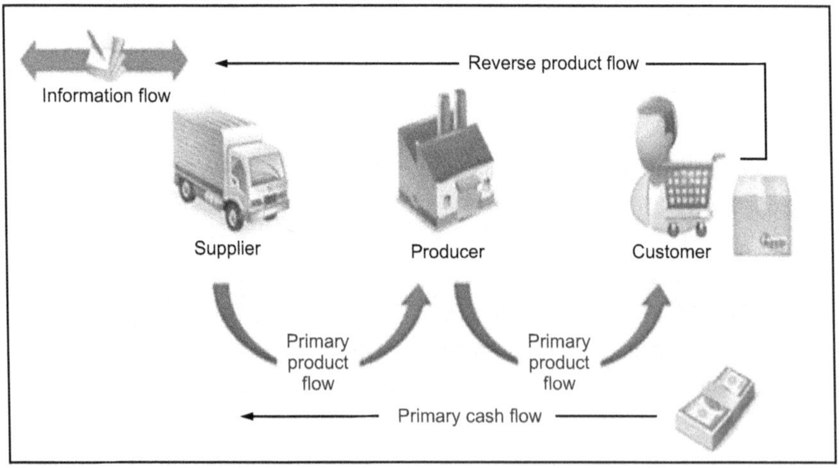

Fig. 2.4: Supply Chain Managemernt Process

- Supply Chain Management might be made up of following organizations:
  - **A Supplier**, a provider of goods or services or a seller with whom the buyer does business. The supplier provides materials, energy, services, or components for use in producing a product or service. These could include items as diverse as sugar cane, fruit,

industrial metals, roofing nails, electric wiring, fabric, computer chips, aircraft turbines, natural gas, electrical power, or transportation services.

- **A Producer**, that receives services, materials, supplies, energy, and components to use in creating finished products, such as dress shirts, packaged dinners, air-planes, electric power, legal counsel, or guided tours.
- **A Customer**, that receives shipments of finished products to deliver to its customers, who wear the shirts, eat the packaged dinners, fly the planes, or turn on the lights.

- An organization's Supply Chain Management or network can have many forms. It can be a simple chain structure with a single strand a complex network, or any structure between those two extremes. No matter whether it is a product or service chain, or what types of entities are involved, companies require their supply chain to guarantee a steady flow of supply while at the same time striving to reduce their supply chain costs. They can improve operating efficiency by employing the right supply chain management structure.

2.3.1 Goals of SCM

1. To cut costs.
2. Increase profits.
3. Improve performance in relationships with customers and suppliers.
4. Develop value added services that give a company a competitive edge.

2.3.2 Functions of SCM

- **Supply Chain Management** involves five main functions: Aligning Flows, Integrating Functions, Coordinating Processes, Designing Complex Systems, and Managing Resources:
    - **Aligning Flows:** As money, materials, and information are passed between customers and suppliers, supply chain management keeps them flowing up and down a supply chain.
    - **Integrating Functions:** Supply Chain Management connects the activities of logistics, purchasing, and operations to ensure that they focus on goals that benefit overall performance.
    - **Coordinating Processes:** Supply Chain Management increases profitability by aligning the processes used to plan, source, make, deliver, and (when necessary) return a company's products and services.

- **Designing Complex Systems:** Simulation tools can predict how a supply chain will behave and show how small changes can cause major disruptions in the flow of materials.
- **Managing Resources:** Supply Chain Managers are responsible for using people, processes, and technology to meet the needs of customers.

2.3.3 Strategies of SCM

- Following are strategies of SCM:
  - **Competitive strategy:** A company's competitive strategy defines, relative to its competitors, the set of customer needs that it seeks to satisfy through its products and services.
  - **Example:** Wal-Mart aims to provide high availability of a variety of products of reasonable quality at low prices.
- **Product development strategy:** It specifies the portfolio of new products that the company will try to develop.
- **Marketing and sales strategy:** It specifies how the market will be segmented and product positioned, priced, and promoted.
- **Supply Chain Strategy:**
  - Determines the nature of material procurement, transportation of materials, manufacture of product or creation of service, distribution of product.
  - Consistency and support between supply chain strategy, competitive strategy, and other functional strategies is important.

2.3.4 Electronic SCM

- E-Supply chain management is practiced in manufacturing industries. E-SCM involves using internet to carry out value added activities so that the products produced by the manufacturer meets customers' and result in good return on investment.
- E-SCM is the effective utilization of internet and business processes that help in delivering goods, services and information from the supplier to the consumer in an organized and efficient way.
- E-SCM is divided into three sub-modules: e-sales, e-stock and e-purchase. Different groups of users are able to access the module through customer portal, agent portal, supplier portal, reseller porter and employee portal, decided by the nature of their work. All participants in the supply chain are able to work collaboratively in purchasing of materials, managing the warehouse and selling the products.

2.3.4.1 Benefits of E-SCM

- Companies implementing E-SCM can has the following benefits:
  1. It improves efficiency.
  2. It reduces inventory.
  3. It reduces cost.
  4. It helps to take competitive advantage over competitors.
  5. It increases ability to implement just-in-time delivery, increases on-time deliveries, which enhances customer satisfaction.
  6. It reduces cycle time, increases revenue, by providing improved customer service.
  7. It improves order fulfillment, order management, decision making, forecasting, demand planning, and warehouse/ distribution activities.
  8. It reduces paperwork, administrative overheads, inventory build-up, and the number of hands that handle goods on their way to the end-user i.e., the customer.

2.3.4.2 Components of Electronic SCM

- The major components of e-SCM are: e-procurement, replenishment systems, collaborative planning, collaborative product design and product development, e-logistics, and supply webs (exchanges).
  - **Supply Chain Replenishment:** Supply chain replenishment encompasses the integrated production and distribution processes. Companies can use replenishment information to reduce inventories, eliminate stocking points, and increase the velocity of replenishment by synchronizing supply and demand information across the extended enterprise.
  - **E-Procurement:** It is the use of web-based technology to support the key procurement processes, including requisitioning, sourcing, contracting, ordering, and payment. E-procurement supports the purchase of both direct and indirect materials and employs several web-based functions, such as online catalogs, contracts, purchase orders, and shipping notices.
  - **Supply Chain Monitoring and Control Using RFID:** This is one of the most promising applications of RFID (Radio-Frequency Identification).
  - **Inventory Management Using Wireless Devices:** Many organizations are now achieving improvements in inventory management by using combinations of bar-coding technologies (or RFID) and wireless devices.
  - **Collaborative Planning:** It is a business practice that combines the business knowledge and forecasts of multiple players along a

supply chain to improve the planning and fulfillment of customer demand. Collaborative planning requires buyers and sellers to develop shared demand forecasts and supply plans for how to support demand.

- **Collaborative Design and Product Development:** It involves the use of product design and development techniques across multiple companies to improve product launch success and reduce time to market. During product development, engineering and design drawings can be shared over a secure network among the contract firm, testing facility, marketing firm, and downstream manufacturing and service companies.
- **E-Logistics:** It is the use of web-based technologies to support the material acquisition, warehousing, and transportation processes. E-logistics enables distribution to couple routing optimization with inventory-tracking information. For example, Internet-based freight auctions enable spot buying of trucking capacity.

2.3.4.3 Major Infrastructure Elements and Tools of e-SCM

- The key activities of e-SCM use a variety of infrastructure and tools. The following are the major infrastructure elements and tools of e-SCM:
    - Electronic data interchange (EDI). It is the major tool used by large corporations to facilitate supply chain relationships. Many companies are shifting from traditional EDI to Internet-based EDI.
    - Its major purpose is to support inter organizational communication and collaboration.
    - These are the corporate internal networks for communication and collaboration.
    - Corporate portals. These provide a gateway for external and internal collaboration, communication, and information search.
    - Workflow systems and tools. These are systems that manage the flow of information in organizations.
    - Groupware and other collaborative tools. Many tools facilitate collaboration and communication between two parties and among members of small as well as large groups. Various tools, some of which are collectively known as groupware, enable such collaboration. Blogs and wikis are beginning to play an important role. A major purpose of these tools is to provide visibility to all, namely, let people know where items are and when they arrive at certain locations.

- o Identification and tracking tools. These tools are designed to identify items and their location along the supply chain.

2.3.4.4 Electronic logistics and its Implementation

- E-logistic is the logistical process that governs everything related to the online marketplace. It is a relatively novel concept. It is a dynamic set of communication computing and collaborative technologies that transform key logistical processes to be customer-centric by sharing data, knowledge and information with supply chain partners. It helps in coping with newly arising logistics challenges.
- The key elements of e-logistics are multi channel operation, cross border functionality, warehouse layout and inventory, planning and forecasting and performance management.
- Success in e-logistics depends on the focus selected for the online shop.
- Proper collaboration, transparent communication with customers for delivery and returns are the other key factors that determines the success of e-logistic.

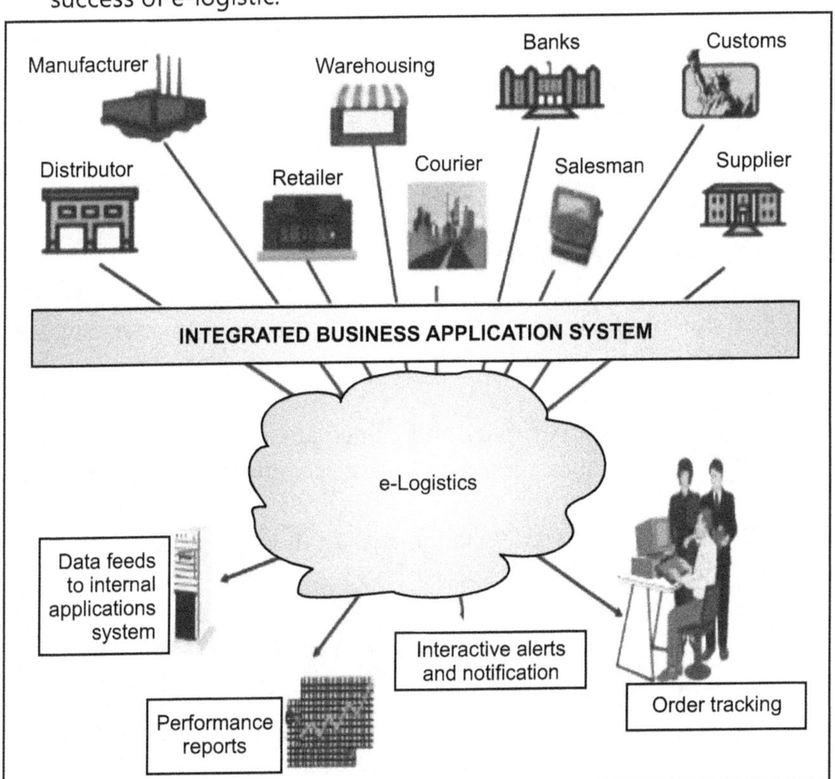

Fig. 2.5: E-Logistics

Process involved in e-logistics (B2C):

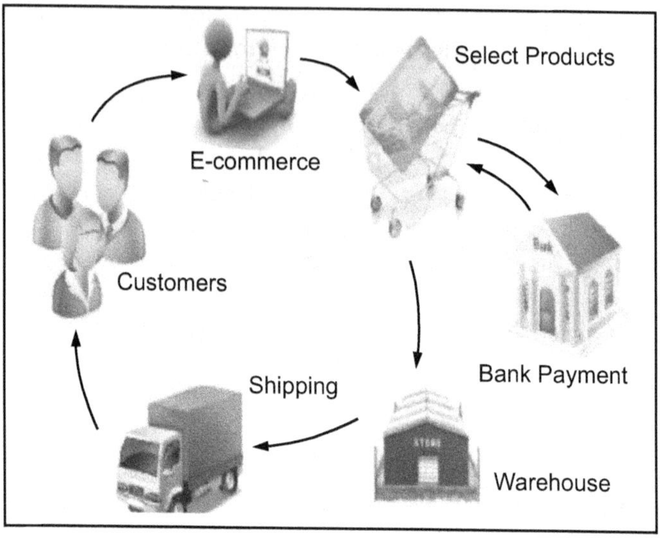

Fig. 2.6: E-logistics process

1. **Method of Payment:**
   Possible payment methods:
   - **At the time of order:** e-payment (e.g. PayPal), Credit Card.
   - **At the time of delivery:** COD.

   For electronic payments, a system of verification of payment is needed before shipping.
2. **Check Product Availability:**
   - If possible, inform customer of availability before order is placed.
   - If out of stock or the product will take time to manufacture, inform customer of the delay.
3. **Arrange Shipments:**
   - Electronic shipping: quick and immediate.
   - Physical product: determine best shipping method level of service.
   - It is the biggest activity (labor, energy, money etc.) for e-logistics.
4. **Insurance:**
   - This option needs to be available for customers since product can be lost or damaged in the shipping process.
5. **Replenishment:**
   - This is an overview step. It should be examining all aspects of physical inventory at allocation and reordering as needed.

- **Product:** Product sitting on shelves or material to manufacture product.
- **Non-product:** Shipping materials, parts for machines in process, items that are part of the shipping process(scanners, carts etc.)

6. Contact with Customers:

- With an invisible process (back-door operations), the customer needs to be informed as much as possible.
- Most common types of communication:
  - Order confirmation
  - Payment success
  - Shipping confirmation
  - Tracking information
  - Any problems in the process.

7. Returns:

- The flow of product from customer back to the vendor is called Reverse Logistics.
- Possible reasons for customers to return or exchange product:
  - Damaged
  - Doesn't work
  - Don't like it.
  - Wrong type/product/color.
  - Implementation of Electronic logistics.

Development of E-Logistics System:

- The development of logistics falls into three stages, namely military logistics, business logistics and e-logistics.
- In which the E-logistics has been the latest word appearing in the logistic industry. Presently the E-logistics has been mostly defined according to the definition of Electronic Logistics, in which the most typical one is that electronic logistics refers to the process which utilizes web technology as an important tool to manage the whole logistic process or some sectors of it.
- Prof. Zhai Xuewei regards E-logistics as the combination of logistics supporting E-Commerce and the electronic technology for logistics. Based on the above definitions and other literature, the author holds that E-logistics, namely E-logistic commerce, which has been characterized with electronic technology, network technology and

automation, can be regarded as the integration of information flow, fund flow and logistical service.

- E-logistics realizes the utility of electronic technology and integration of logistic organization, trade, management and service modes. It is entitled to share data, knowledge and other information with partners in the supply chain. Seen from these definitions, as E-logistics has been combined with the meaning of commerce, then it is also equipped with the same procedure of commerce from negotiation, contract signoff, payment, and implementation to balance counting and utilizes electronic technology in each step.

The Development Patterns of E-Logistics:

- Development patterns of E-logistics are divided into two categories. The first one is defined in the E-logistic information market which is a new information system established on Internet.
- In this pattern, the information about the logistics information of the consignor or about the usable vehicles of transportation companies can be input on the Internet and both the parties can sign a contract in accordance with this information.
- In other words, the consignor can put such information involving transferred goods categories, quantities and destinations on Internet and the transportation company can provide related information (such as the location of usable vehicles) to the consignor through Internet; and then based on the above information both the parties can sign a contract.
- The main functions of this pattern include information search, dissemination and bid; other functions mainly refer to providing such services as industry information, goods insurance, logistic tracing, road condition and GPS.
- For example, National Transportation Trade Market (www.Net.net), as an electronic transportation market, builds a trade Internet for the consignor, the logistic company and the transporter through Internet technology.
- The second pattern is based on an E-logistic system specialized in providing supply chain management for logistic enterprises. It is characterized by electronic technology, which utilizes Internet to complete the coordination, monitoring and management of the whole logistic process and provide all mediate services between Internet foregrounding and end customers.

- Typically, this pattern combines various software technologies and logistic services, in which way the close link among fund flow, logistics and information flow can be completed.
- This type of link can provide visibility among enterprises, which enables these enterprises to control and manage storage to a maximum extent. Meanwhile, with the aids of such advanced information technologies as customer management system, the integration of commercial intelligent computers and telephones, geographical information system, GPS, Internet and wireless net technology as well as such logistics management technology and modes as rationing optimization. Dynamic monitoring, intelligent transportation and storage optimization, the E-logistics provides an advanced and integrated management system and then enables enterprises to establish supply chain system as soon as possible.
- It can be imagined that without electronic technology, it is impossible for all participates in the supply chain to operate regularly when they have to receive thousands of cases involving hundreds of suppliers and retailers.

E-Logistics Processes:

- When it comes to logistics, the challenge has always been how to deliver products to customers as quickly as possible.
- Logistics is concerned with the flow of materials in the supply chain, from source through the industrial process to the customer, and then on to reuse/recycle or disposal.
- By coordinating all resources, logistics have to ensure that service levels agreements with customers are honored.
- E-logistics is defined to be the mechanism of automating logistics processes and providing an integrated, end-to-end fulfillment and supply chain management services to the players of logistics processes.
- Those logistics processes that are automated by E-logistics provide supply chain visibility and can be part of existing e-Commerce or Workflow systems in an enterprise.
- The typical E-logistics processes include Request For Quotes (RFQ), Shipping, and Tracking. As shown in Fig. 2.7, E-Logistics interacts with the business process manager in an e-Commerce server.

E-logistics Model Framework:

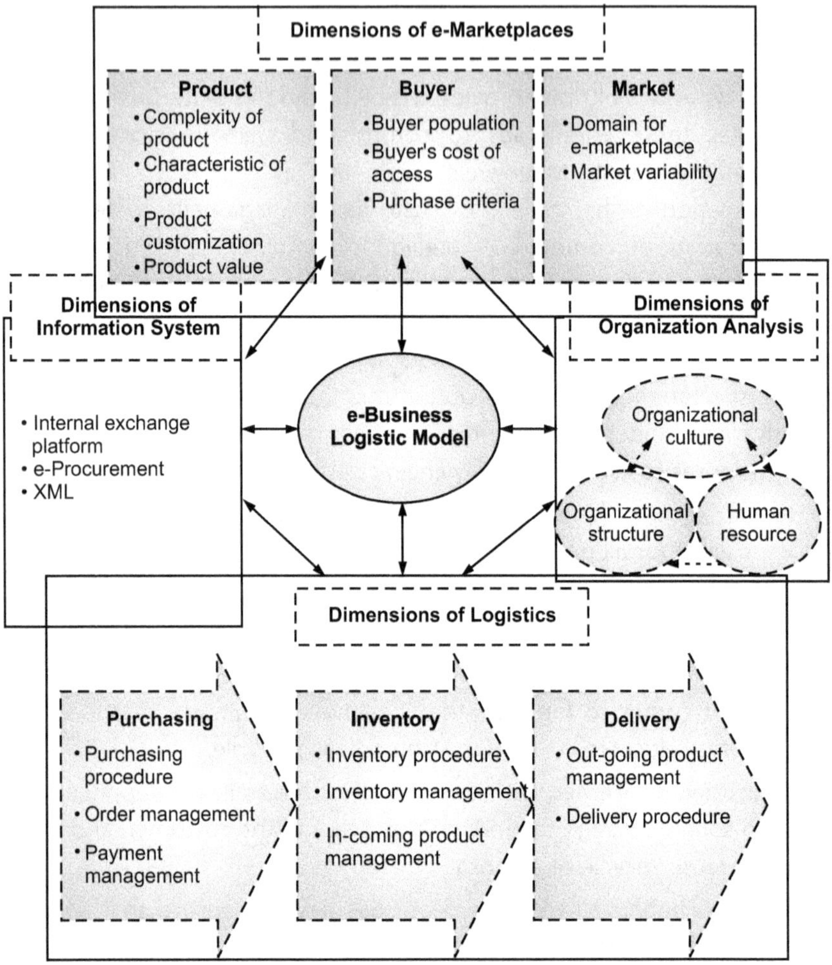

Fig. 2.7: An E-Business Mode for the Logistic Industry

- The business process manager invokes the RFQ process to get the basic services such as getting the quotes in an E-logistics process.
- Whenever the response is obtained, the purchase order (PO) is updated. Shipping process is also invoked by the business process manager and upon completion updates the PO.
- Once goods are shipped, the tracking number is given to the customer and that tracking number is mapped to the PO number in an E-Commerce system.
- Customers can track their shipment with the help of that number.

SUMMARY

- E-Marketing also known as online or internet advertising which uses the internet technology to promote online message to customer. E-Marketing examples are e-mail or social media advertising, web banners and mobile advertising.
- Goals associated with effective web sites include: Attracting visitors. Making the site interesting to explore. Creating a positive image consistent with the company's desires. Reinforcing already held positive images regarding the company.
- Website maintenance is the act of regularly checking your website for issues and mistakes and keeping it updated and relevant.
- Online marketing is a set of tools and methodologies used for promoting products and services through the internet. The methods and techniques used for online marketing include e-mail, social media, display advertising, search engine optimization, Google AdWords and more
- Customer Relationship Management (CRM) refers to the principles, practices, and guidelines that an organization follows when interacting with its customers.
- Electronic Customer Relationship Management (E-CRM) is the application of Internet-based technologies such as e-mails, websites, chat rooms, forums and other channels to achieve CRM objectives.
- Supply Chain Management (SCM) is a systems approach to managing the entire flow of information, materials, and services from raw materials suppliers through factories and warehouses to the end customer.
- E-Logistics is the logical process that governs everything related to the online market place.

CHECK YOUR UNDERSTANDING

1. ______ is the process of marketing accomplished or facilitated via the use of internet technologies (e.g. web, e-mail, intranet, extranets).
   (a) Internet marketing (b) Search marketing
   (c) e-marketing (d) Mobile marketing
2. What does CRM stand for?
   (a) Consumer Relations Management
   (b) Customer Relationship Marketing
   (c) Customer Relationship Management
   (d) Consumer Returns Management

3. Which of the following is true for supply chain management?
   (a) The physical material moves in the direction of the end of chain
   (b) Flow of cash backwards through the chain
   (c) Exchange of information moves in both the direction
   (d) All of the above
4. Which are traditional marketing strategy.
   (a) Telephone (b) Direct mail
   (c) Broadcast (d) All of the above
5. What is the full form of word (e-CRM).
   (a) electronic Customer Relationship Management.
   (b) e-mail customer Relationship Management.
   (c) electronic Consumer Relationship Management.
   (d) electronic Customer Review Management.

Answers

1. (c)	2. (c)	3. (d)	4. (d)	5. (a)

PRACTICE QUESTIONS

1. Answers the Following Question in brief:

7. Define e-marketing.
7. Which are the metrics to define internet units of measurement.
7. Write short note on CRM processes
7. Which are goals of SCM.
7. What is an electronic logistics?

2. Answer the Following Questions:

5. What is the difference between traditional marketing and e-marketing?
5. What is online marketing? Explain with its advantages.
5. What is marketing automation?
5. Write architecture and applications of E-CRM?

3. Write short note on:

e-marketing, Site adhesion, Website, Online marketing, CRM, SCM, Electronic SCM, Web presence, Hits, page views, E-Logistics.

4. Answer True or False:

25. Video Marketing is a type of E-Marketing.
25. Newspaper, magazines are traditional marketing strategy.
25. Keep a regular backup schedule is a regular website maintenance task.
25. Service and Marketing are not key business process areas of CRM.
25. E-logistic is the logistical process that governs everything related to the online marketplace.

Answers

1. (T)	2. (T)	3. (T)	4. (F)	5. (T)

■■■

Unit **3**...

Electronic Payment System

Objectives ...

- To understand concept of EPS.
- To know about EDI and its Architecture.
- To get information about Digital Signature and Digital Certificate.
- To learn about Online Payment Systems.

3.1 ELECTRONIC DATA INTERFACE

- In this section, we will learn about EDI and its architecture, financial EDI and overview of the technology of EDI.

3.1.1 Introduction to EDI

- EDI stands for Electronic Data Interchange. Electronic Data Interchange is a system which allows document information to be communicated between businesses, government's structures and other entities.
- Electronic data interchange is a method for transferring data between different computer systems or computer networks. It is commonly used by big companies for e-commerce purposes, such as sending orders to warehouses or tracking their order.
- EDI is the direct computer to computer exchange between two organisations or companies of standard business transaction documents, such as invoices, payments, purchase orders, shipping orders etc.
- Electronic data interchange (EDI) is the structured transmission of data between organisations by electronic means.
- EDI is used to transfer electronic documents or business data from one computer system to another computer system, i.e. from one trading partner to another trading partner without human intervention.
- In EDI information is passed electronically from one computer to another over a network without having to the read, retyped or printed.

- The information transferred must have a standard defined structure agreed between every company and the company user who send and receive data from that company.

What is EDI?

- Electronic Data Interchange (EDI) is the computer-to-computer exchange of routine business data between trading partners in standard electronic formats.
- This definition contains 3 key concepts about EDI:
  1. **Computer-to-computer:** EDI in its most efficient form flows directly out of a sender's computer system directly into a receiver's computer system without any human intervention; however, it is not always possible for EDI to flow in this most efficient manner.
  2. **Routing business documents:** EDI is used for routine business documents like Purchase Orders and Invoices. It is not used for non-routine business documents like complicated contracts or information meant for humans to read and analyze.
  3. **Standard data formats:** A standard definition of the location and structure of the data is provided. Unstructured text is not used in EDI.
- The Fig. 3.1 illustrates how much slower the conventional paper process than the EDI process. Additionally, the conventional paper process includes substantially more human intervention to move business information from one company to another.

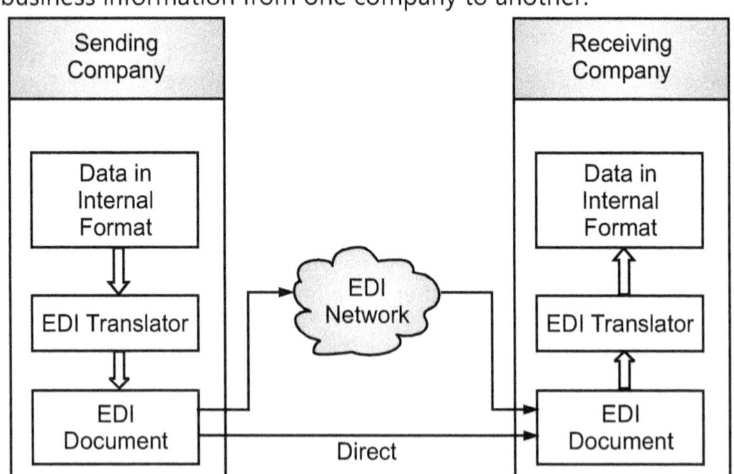

Fig. 3.1: EDI process Vs Conventional paper process

- The conventional process requires someone to handle a printed computer generated form and mail it. Then, the recipient re-keys the data back into another computer for their internal processing. The EDI process is one computer transmitting the information directly to another computer, eliminating the paperwork and human intervention.

Definition of EDI:

- We can define Electronic Data Interchange (EDI) as "the exchange of business data from one organisation's computer application to the computer application of a trading partner".

OR

- EDI (Electronic Data Interchange) is a standard format for exchanging business data.

OR

- EDI is a standardized method for transferring data between different computer systems or computer networks. EDI is commonly used for e-commerce purposes, such as sending orders to warehouses, tracking shipments, and creating invoices.

OR

- EDI is a set of protocols for conducting electronic business over computer networks.

3.1.2 EDI Model

- EDI Model involves trading partners who wants to exchange data from the organisations or companies.
  There may be two companies or firms with a common customer or two banks whose customers wants to deal with one another or between two divisions of the same company or firm, although if they have an integrated computer system, normally this would not be treated as EDI.
- Trading partners will have the flow of data between them through exchanges.
- The simplest and the most common form of exchange is where one partner wants to send a single message to the other and to know whether or not the message is received by the other.
- Further, exchanges may be sequential messages following the first one, in some way linked to the first which would be part of the same exchange. For example, the telephone conversation carried on by telephone answering machine between two people who are not present when the other calls.

- The exchange is divided into messages on which most EDI standards concentrate.
- The message is passed successfully and reliably from one partner to the other, it is said EDI is operated.
- The message has an originator who is the creator of the message and a destination which is the other trading partner.
- There may be one message to reach several destinations, though the procotol of the EDI system usually not permit this.

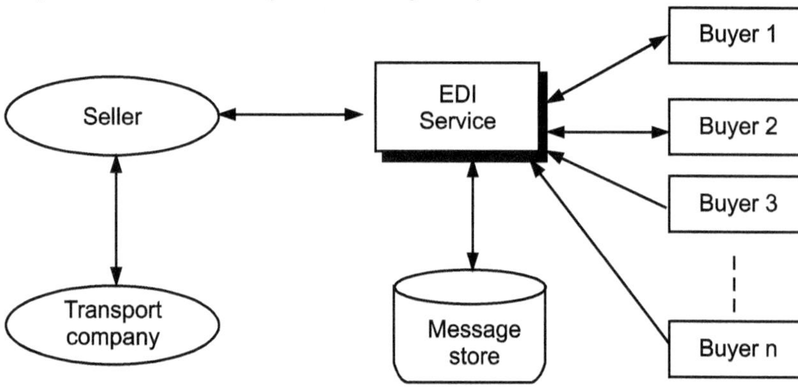

Fig. 3.2: EDI Model

3.1.3 How EDI Works?

- For the most part, EDI-based transactions are really the same as their manual, paper counterparts. The difference is that the EDI transactions are sent and received electronically, as packets of data formatted according to EDI standards.
- There are effectively three major processes involved in the exchange of EDI data: Mapping, Translation and Communications.
  1. **Mapping** involves transforming an EDI document into another format (such as XML, a flat file, a delimited file, etc.) or vice versa. Mapping is essential for proper system integration.
  2. **Translation** is the process of accepting inbound EDI data, or preparing an outbound file for transmission.
  3. **Communications** refers to the transmission of the EDI transaction. This can be done indirectly, through an external clearing house or VAN ("Value Added Network") or direct via AS2 using EDI software, a web-based EDI tool or outsourcing with an EDI Service Provider.

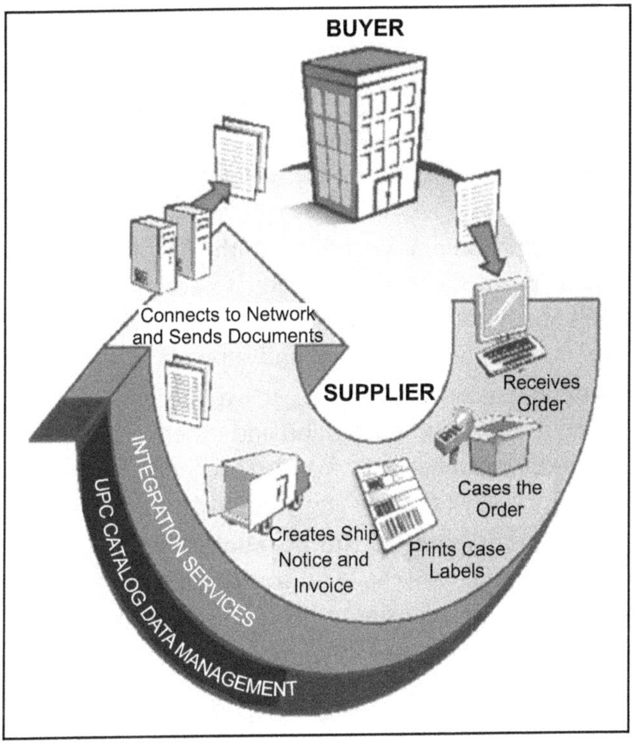

Fig. 3.3: EDI in Retail Environment

- **For example:** The EDI process work in the retail environment.
- The retailer will initiate the process with an electronic transmission of an electronic Purchase Order (850). The supplier will receive the order, case it and print UCC-128 labels. Then, the order is packed and the UCC-128 labels are placed on the cartons.
- The cartons are then shipped to the retailer and the supplier electronically transmits an Advanced Ship Notice (856). After the shipment has been sent, the supplier transmits an electronic Invoice (810) for the goods.
- These electronic documents are sent in a standard Electronic Data Interchange (EDI) format.

3.1.4 Advantages

- The advantages of EDI are:
  1. **Lower costs:** By reducing the manual keying of data, handling of documents and other processes, you can potentially reduce the costs of labor and paper, and reduce errors (and their associated costs).

2. **Higher efficiency:** Sending and receiving EDI data happens in seconds, and the information can be acted on immediately. This means time savings for you and your trading partners.
3. **Improved accuracy:** You can reduce errors by using EDI because manual and duplicate entry is eliminated. Everything flows untouched, leaving a trail for easy future tracking.
4. **More supply chain visibility:** With EDI, product sales data, product inventory status, demand forecasts and other metrics can be shared with suppliers and their suppliers. This allows for better inventory management and supports just-in-time delivery.
5. **Enhanced security:** Thanks to numerous communications protocols addressing encryption and other security issues, critical business or personal data may be exchanged with higher levels of security via EDI than by any other means.
6. **Greater management information:** Because EDI data is electronic data, you have a source of information to guide management decisions or to mine for further analysis.
7. **Improvements in overall data quality:** Using EDI we keep better record keeping, fewer errors in data, reduction in processing time, less reliance on human interpretation of data, minimized unproductive time and so on.
8. **Reduces paperwork:** The EDI process can be handled without using a single piece of paper. It reduces expenses of storage, printing, postage, mailing and recycling.
9. **Availability of data in electronic form:** Data from EDI is in electronic form, which makes it easy to share across the organisations.
10. **Reduces data entry errors:** With EDI data goes directly from one computer to another computer without involving a human being.

3.1.5 Disadvantages

- Disadvantages of EDI are as given below:
  1. **High cost:** Applications development in EDI is costly.
  2. **Multiple Standards:** There are too many standards bodies developing standard documents formats for EDI. For example your company may be following the X12 standard format, while its trading partner follows the EDIFACT standard format.

3. **Changing Standards:** Each year, most standards bodies publish revisions to the standards. This poses a problem to EDI users. You may be using one version of the standard while your trading partners are still using older versions.
4. **Too Expensive:** Some companies are only doing business with others who use EDI. If a company wants to do business with these organisations, they have to implement an EDI program. This expense may be very costly for small companies.
5. **Limit Your Trading Partners:** Some large companies tend to stop doing business with companies who don't comply with EDI. For example Wal Mart is only doing business with other companies that use EDI. The result of this is a limited group of people you can do business with.
6. **Less transparent:** EDI is less transparent than paper-based systems.
7. **Structured Method:** EDI is a structured way of working, companies usually change operating procedures.

3.2 EDI E-COMMERCE BASIC ARCHITECTURE

- EDI architecture provides a framework that enables you to standardize the information which can be easily exchanged between and within business organizations and government entities using electronic channels.

EDI Layered Architecture:

- The architecture of EDI is divided into four layers:
  1. Application (Semantic) Layer
  2. Standards Translation Layer
  3. Transport (Packing) Layer
  4. Physical Network Infrastructure Layer

1. Application Layer:

- The first layer of EDI defines the business applications that are used by EDI. This layer of EDI translates business application into request for quotes, purchase orders, acknowledgement and invoices. For every company this layer is specific and also for the software that company uses.
- The application layer also called the semantic layer.

- This layer is specific to a company and the software it uses, i.e. the user interface and content visible on the screen are tailored or customized to local environment.
- By the semantic layer of the EDI the companies from are change into more specific format and then it may be send to various partners of the company have a several software applications to handle all forms aspects.
- To achieve all above activities the company must follow to EDI standard example of EDI standards are X12, ANSI, EDIFACT etc. If the sender and receivers of company want to exchange some files then requires a compatible standards of Electronic Data Interchange.
- The sender who want to send a data use a software application with EDI and exchange data in EDI format so that at the receivers end the receiver can read it. The EDI standards are very important in exchange of data because at sending end a sender manipulate data by EDI as in receiving end data is manipulated by EDI.

2. Standard Layer:

- This layer of EDI architecture defines the structure of the business form and some content which are related with the application layer.
- This layer of EDI has no mean without application layer so we can say that EDI applications and standard layer are interlinked.

3. Transport Layer:

- EDI transport layer is a non-electronic way of sending the business form from one company to another company.
- This non-electronic way may be registered mail, postal services or private career, telecommunications, fax etc. Now-a-days, the transportation method is more complex with compare to e-mail.

4. Physical Layer:

- The physical layer of EDI also called the infrastructure layer.
- This layer defined the component communication path of EDI data transaction. What are the structure of e-commerce supported EDI in which information can be build and what are the communication established over which EDI data transfer from one customer to another customer.

3.3 FINANCIAL EDI

- Financial EDI is the electronic transfer of payments, payment - related information, or other financial documents in a standardized, machine - readable format.
- The electronic exchange of financial information closes the transaction chain and fully integrates the business process with payment handling and accounting.
- FEDI, together with EDI, constitutes an integrated electronic business process that enables business organisations to automate their entire operation from order and acquisition to payment and accounting.
- A simple definition is that FEDI is "a tool for the payment cycle, but in a larger perspective".
- The goal of financial logistics is to make relevant financial resources available at the right time to the right business partner.
- Payments based on EDI are a first step in the implementation of financial logistics. Quick, automated financial services are an important component in the EDI-based business process.
- We can say that, from the functional point of view, both methods of electronic document exchange are principally equivalent (a slightly modified home-banking server is often used).
- FEDI's advantage is absolutely indisputable if the bank client uses EDI tools for other business processes.

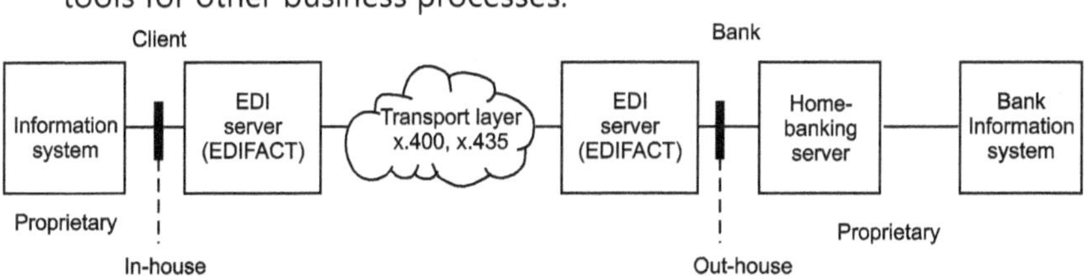

Fig. 3.4: A schematic presentation of a FEDI system

How does Financial EDI Work?

- To send a payment through financial EDI, there are a few steps that a company or institution undertakes.

  Step 1 : The buyer electronically extracts payment information from the organization's accounts payable system.

  Step 2 : That data is formatted into an EDI standard.

  Step 3 : Then, the transaction set is transmitted to the organization's bank.

Step 4 : Next, the bank formats that information into the format necessary for its transmission through the Automated Clearing House (ACH) Network as an ACH transaction.

Step 5 : The ACH network delivers the payment and its associated data to the seller's bank, with the bank crediting the seller.

Step 6 : It automatically transmits the payment information to the seller's accounts receivable system.

The strategic advantages of FEDI include:

1. The extension of service offered by increasing the level of in-time and detailed information (the basis for offering attractive new services).
2. An easier way of coupling payments and settling claims among business partners.
3. A competitive advantage in the banking sector and a way of bank differentiation from the client's point of view.
4. Better managerial information.
5. An increased security level.
6. A payer can generate payment from his in-house system in the same manner for all banks.
7. Partners are not too dependent on each other as open standards are used.
8. An easier way of finding and storing data.
9. Reductions in operating expenses.

3.4 OVERVIEW OF THE TECHNOLOGY INVOLVED IN EDI

1. Data Processing and EDI:

- One of the technological fields required to implement EDI is data processing.
- Data processing allows the EDI operation to take information that is resident in a user application and transform that data into a format that is recognizable to all other user applications that have an interest in using the data. In the EDI environment, data processing will handle both outgoing and incoming data, as depicted in Fig. 3.6.

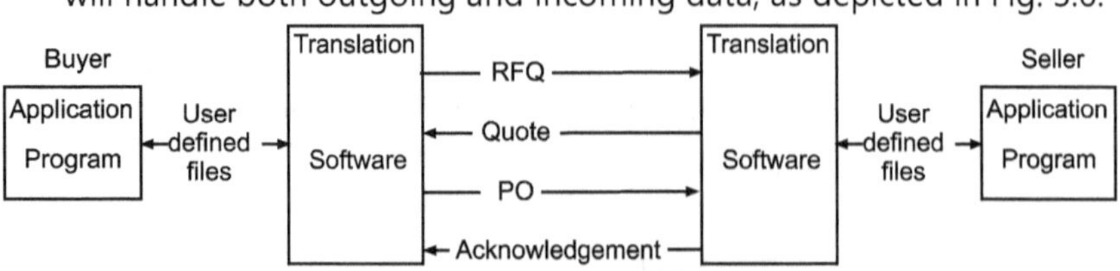

Fig. 3.5: Data Processing and EDI

- The user-defined files in Fig. 3.5 are the flat files that are produced by a business application. These files may or may not be formatted by the user. These are the business files that need to be translated into the X12 format.
- The translation software in Fig. 3.5 is the software that maps the elements of a user-defined file into the ANSI X12 or EDIFACT standard format. This software is available through commercial retailers on various platforms from PCs to mainframes.
- The mapping of the user-defined data elements into the translation software requires some skill in mapping. The mapping itself requires knowledge of both the translation software and the EDI standards being used so new mapping and processing rules can be set up for the translator.
- If a new trading partner places no new requirements on the translator, the new trading partner is simply set up under existing mapping rules. However, when the trading partner requires that additional or different data fields to be sent, a new mapping scheme needs to be identified and associated with that trading partner.

2. Data communications and EDI:

- The other technological field that is heavily involved in EDI implementation is data communications. Once the standards have been employed and the required software is in place, the EDI participant still needs to have the ability to communicate with remote trading partners to take advantage of EDI.

(i) Transport mechanisms move the data:

- Data must be transported across telecommunications lines in order for the trading partners to trade information.
- Some basic concepts that describe mechanisms and methods used in this transport of data:
  - (a) Direct connect is the term used to indicate that two EDI trading partners trade information directly to each other without a third-party connection service. Direct connects are normally used by large corporations for intracompany EDI transactions and for intercompany transactions with trading partners that have established high-volume rates of exchange of EDI data.
  - (b) Modems are heavily used by EDI practitioners today. Modem-to-modem connections provide a level of security and reliability that long-time practitioners are reluctant to give up. The standard in

the industry, as this paper is written, is transmission by binary synchronous modem or bisync. This method allows for high-speed continuous transmission in which the sending and receiving modems are controlled by clock pulses. The clock pulses regulate the rate and timing of the data flow.

(c) Routers, although not the primary transport mechanism for EDI transactions today, have the potential to become the de facto standard of transmission for high-volume traffic. Currently, routers are used mainly over leased lines, requiring expensive setups and ongoing data communications transport costs.

(ii) Communications protocols standardize the data formats:

- EDI transactions can be passed between trading partners using standard transmission protocols. Graphic images, charts, and diagrams must be transmitted using protocols that allow the transfer of binary data.
- Some of these common standards are SMTP, MIME, X.400, X.435, and X.500. Internet Protocols are excluded from this discussion as the audience is already very familiar with them.

(a) X.400 is an electronic messaging standard that was developed by the Consultative Committee on International Telegraph and Telephone, which is tasked with developing standards to enable incompatible networks and computer systems to exchange data.

(b) X.435 is a standard that further enhances the X.400 standard to make it deal more effectively with EDI transmission requirements. X.435 is the specification for the EDI body part that attaches to the X.400 message.

(c) X.500 is an addressing directory containing the names and characteristics of electronic messaging receivers. X.500 facilitates the delivery of X.400 messages, including those that include the X.435 standard. The idea is the production of a global electronic directory and a guide to associated databases so the user can find an e-mail address if it is needed and not known.

3.5 INTRODUCTION OF EPS

Introduction of Online Payment System:

- An online payment system is an Internet-based method of processing economic transactions. It allows a vendor to accept payments over the web or over other Internet connections, such as direct database connections between retail stores and their suppliers--a common method of maintaining just-in-time inventories. Online payment systems greatly expand the reach of a business and its ability to make sales.

Facts:

- Online payment systems typically are run by third-party corporations, such as PayPal, Google or Click2Pay. These companies make a profit by taking a small percentage of every transaction, or by signing contracts with institutions that need to make a large number of transactions.

Significance:

- A large Internet storefront, such as Amazon.com, could not exist without the ability to take online payments. Online payment systems have leveled the playing field between large and small companies, as any of them can accept the same payment methods once they sign up with third-party payment processors.

Geography:

- The reach of online payment is as large as the Internet, but many payment methods are restricted by national law or by the unwillingness of some vendors and consumers to work with residents of countries where national regulation is lax. For example, Nigeria is infamous for having no enforceable fraud protection, which leads many vendors to disallow transactions originating from that country.

Considerations:

- There are very few businesses that cannot benefit from participating in an online payment system. However, because these transactions are through third-party vendors, no business should rely entirely on a single supplier for online transactions. Diversification in the use of online payment systems is key to ensuring that a business's cash flow is not interrupted by problems with a single vendor.

3.5.1 Definition

- Electronic Payment System (EPS) is a system which helps the user or customer to make online payments.

OR

- The term electronic payment can refer narrowly to e-commerce - a payment for buying and selling goods or services offered through the internet.

3.5.2 Application of Online Payment

- Following are business applications that one may get after implementing online invoice payment to his/her business:
  1. **Instant Payment:** Online invoice payment is is quick and hassle-free payment. One can easily make a payment sitting comfortably at home or office. The gateway to accept payment online provides the instant notification of the transaction that makes the customer remain assured of the purchased items.
  2. **Quick and Easy Setup:** Setting up an option to receive online payment is easy and quick to start selling minutes after implementing it. Moreover, there are many service providers that offers affordable plans with zero setup fee and very low transaction rates.
  3. **Credibility for Merchants:** An online invoice software with features to receive online payment is more secure and credible for merchants than receiving payments through cheques. A merchant instantly receives the money with no risk of bounced cheques and the fees associated with it.
  4. **Merchant Reliability:** Customers today often consider merchants more reliable that accept payment online through their site. It encourages them to do business with the merchant. At the same time, online invoice payment offers consumer with the fraud protection that secures their money if they don't receive the product purchased online through a website.
  5. **Recurring Payments:** Online payment could be more suitable if you are offering some subscription-based services where your users/customers need to make payments after a certain period of time. Instead of sending them reminders every time and requesting to send cheques for the payment, you can automatically collect payments after the end of the subscription term.
  6. **Credit Card Payments:** Customers can use their credit cards to make payments, even though they don't have money in their bank account. You can break down the payment into several installments, if you are selling expensive items. And one can use credit cards to pay you in installments.
  7. **Affiliate Marketing:** If you have an online invoice payment system in place, you can create an affiliate program where your

affiliates can earn referral commissions by sending buyers to you. This will boost your sales and can find an affiliate network, working to increase your revenue.

8. **Getting a competitive edge:** For a merchant, an option to receive online payment can improve reputation, allowing it to gain the trust of the customers. Moreover, when others have online payment systems, you cannot afford to ask for payments via cheques.
9. **Influences buyers:** An online invoice payment method may influence customers to purchase items listed on the website. Since the transaction is quick and easy, and one can pay via credit cards.
10. **Last minute deals:** Many times, merchants throw cost-saving deals to attract customers. If you can receive online payment on your site, a customer can take hold of a deal even at the last minute. This will increase sales.

3.5.3 Advantages and Disadvantages of E-Payment

- Electronic payment allows your customers to make cashless payments for goods and services through cards, mobile phones or the internet. It presents a number of advantages, including cost and time savings, increased sales and reduced transaction costs. But it is vulnerable to internet fraud and could potentially increase business expenses.

Advantages:

1. **Increased Speed and Convenience:** E-payment is very convenient compared to traditional payment methods such as cash or cheque. Since you can pay for goods or services online at any time of day or night, from any part of the world, your customers don't have to spend time in a line, waiting for their turn to transact. Nor do they have to wait for a check to clear the bank so they can access the funds they need to shop. E-payment also eliminates the security risks that come with handling cash money.
2. **Increased Sales:** As internet banking and shopping become widespread, the number of people making cash payments is decreasing. According to Bankrate, more than two-thirds of consumers carry less than $50 a day, meaning electronic alternatives are increasingly becoming the preferred payment

option. As such, e-payment enables businesses to make sales to the customers who choose to pay electronically and gain a competitive advantage over those that only accept traditional methods.

3. **Reduced Transaction Costs:** While there are no additional charges for making a cash payment, trips to the store typically cost money, and cheques also need postage. On the other hand, there are usually no fees or very small ones to swipe your card or pay online. In the long run, e-payment could save both individuals and businesses hundreds to thousands of dollars in transaction fees.

Disadvantages:

1. **Security Concerns:** Measures such as symmetric encryption are in place to make e-payment safe and secure, it is still vulnerable to hacking. Fraudsters, for instance, use phishing attacks to trick unsuspecting users into providing the log-in details of their e-wallets, which they capture and use to access the victims' personal and financial information. Inadequate authentication also troubles e-payment systems. Without superior identity verification measures like biometrics and facial recognition, anyone can use another person's cards and e-wallets and get away without being caught. These security concerns may make some people against to use e-payment systems.
2. **Disputed Transactions:** If someone uses your company's electronic money without your authorization, you would identify the unfamiliar charge and file a claim with your bank, online payment processor or credit card company. Without sufficient information about the person who performed the transaction, though, it can be difficult to win the claim and receive a refund.
3. **Increased Business Costs:** E-payment systems come with an increased need to protect sensitive financial information stored in a business's computer systems from unauthorized access. Enterprises with in-house e-payment systems must cause additional costs in procuring, installing and maintaining sophisticated payment-security technologies.

3.5.4 Introduction to EFT (Electronic Fund Transfer)

- EFT stands for Electronic Funds Transfer. EFT is a system of transferring money from one bank account directly to another without any paper money changing hands.
- One of the most widely-used EFT programs is Direct Deposit, in which payroll is deposited straight into an employee's bank account, although EFT refers to any transfer of funds initiated through an electronic terminal, including credit card, ATM, Fedwire and Point-Of-Sale (POS) transactions.
- It is used for both credit transfers, such as payroll payments, and for debit transfers, such as mortgage payments.

3.5.4.1 Definition

- Various definitions of EFT are:
  - Electronic Funds Transfer (EFT) is the paperless act of transmitting money through a computer network.

    OR
  - Electronic funds transfer (EFT) is the electronic exchange, transfer of money from one account to another, either within a single financial institution or across multiple institutions, through computer-based systems.

    OR
  - Electronic funds transfer means the online and computer transfer of money from one bank account to other bank account.

    OR
  - **EFT (Electronic funds transfer)** is the electronic exchange, transfer of money from one account to another, either within a single financial institution or across multiple institutions, through computer-based systems.

3.5.4.2 Basic Concept

- Use of technology in the field of banking could be registered with the beginning of MICR(Magnetic Ink Character Recognition)cheques.
- These cheques were introduced with the objective of ensuring faster clearing. The MICR technology is based on the system of coded language. Each individual instrument (cheque) carries an MICR code line.

- This MICR code line contains numbers. These numbers indicate:
  1. First 6 digits conveying the cheque number.
  2. The next 9 digits are broken into 3 parts of 3 digits each. The first three digits stand for city code, next three for the bank code and the last three signify the branch code.
  3. To the right of these 9 digits are two digits with a reasonable gap between the two. These two digits stand for the type of account i.e. whether savings, current or cash credit etc.
- Coding of such comprehensive information in a single line enables quick sorting of cheques as per their drawee branch and city. This helps the bankers to claim their money quickly from the concerned bankers.
- Banks used reader sorters to ensure that the instruments are sorted on the basis of the information (data) captured in the MICR code line.
- The bankers use the same MICR code line to encode the information mentioned in the cheque.
- The collecting banker is required to sort these cheques as per the claims and these duly sorted and processed instruments are exchanged through the clearing house to reach the drawee bank.
- The process of clearing becomes quick due to the ability of the bankers to present their claims fast on account of MICR technology.
- Technological development led to the introduction of the following:
  1. EFT (Electronic Funds Transfer).
  2. ECS (Electronic Clearing System).
  3. RTGS (Real Time Gross Settlement).
- Electronic funds transfer is a system in which funds are electronically transferred from one bank account to another within 48 hours. The customer gives authority to a banker to debit his account.
- There is a wide variety of users of EFT techniques.
- Other uses often required Automated Clearing Houses (ACHs).
- One of the first uses was for the transfer of computerised credit card clearing information.
- The most sophisticated EFT operations are geared to ACH's and it can provide either credit or debit transfers.

Credit transfers : The initiating institution sends funds through the system to be deposited in the recipient's account.

Debit transfers : The initiating institution withdraws funds from the depositor's account.

- It is similar to standing instructions given by the customer to his bank. The customer has to sign a form that authorises his bank to deduct payment on a certain date.
- He/She is required to give details such as beneficiaries account number, the amount to be deducted and other details of payment. This information is programmed into his/her account.
- As per this instruction on a specified date customer's account is debited and beneficiaries account is credited.
- An electronic fund transfer involves transfer of funds taking the help of computers, and telecommunication.
- Any transaction in bank that involves a transfer that too via an electronic mode should be treated as Electronic Funds Transfers. This transfer could be a debit entry or a credit entry.

3.5.4.3 Types of EFT

- The variants of electronic funds transfer are:
  1. Electronic Clearing System (ECS).
  2. Real Time Gross Settlement (RTGS).
  3. National Electronic Fund Transfer (NEFT).

1. Electronic Clearing System (ECS):

- Electronic clearing system is an improved version of advanced paper based payment system.
- Now ECS is very commonly resorted to, where payments are in bulk and are to be made to large number of people.
- The frequency of such payment is another factor that led to introduction of a system like electronic clearing system.
- Examples are: payment of interest and dividend by companies, payment of income tax refund, salaries etc.,
- The paying agencies prefer the electronic route over the manual route. The reason behind their preferences for electronic route is the drawbacks associated with the paper based payment system.

- Drawbacks of paper based payment system are as follows:
  1. Paper based payment system involves drawing/printing of an instrument, signing of the same, dispatching them to the respective beneficiaries and ensuring that all claims/liabilities are cleared through the drawer's bank. The efforts involved in this process are too much and it is not as cost effective as the existing electronic clearing system.
  2. Paper based system also requires preservation of these documents which is difficult.
  3. The instruments dispatched by the drawer could be lost in transit and are also prone to material alterations. Therefore, an option to the paper based payment system came in the form of electronic clearing system.
- Electronic Clearing System involves transfer of data, which enables transfer of funds from the user of this service to the beneficiaries.
- It is very clear from the preceding discussion that ECS has been introduced because of the time and formalities involved in paper based clearing system.
- With growth of trade and business, the paper based clearing system was turning slow. Hence, quick transfer of funds was essential which came in the form of the Electronic Clearing System.

Parties involved in Electronic Clearing System are:

- Let us understand that since clearing is a function of the Central Bank, the role of Central Bank in an electronic fund transfer is necessary. In fact, the Central Bank facilitates such transfer of funds.
- The other parties to ECS are the user of the service and the beneficiary.
- The user of the service is the person, institution, organisation that would want to transfer, or credit money and beneficiary would be one who would receive the money from the user.
- The user of this service could also be termed as the subscriber. The subscriber would obviously involve his bank called the sponsor bank in it.
- So we have:
  1. The clearing bank (RBI).
  2. The user of the service (the subscriber).
  3. The user's bank (sponsor bank).
  4. The beneficiary(who receives the payment).

- **The working of the Electronic Clearing System:** There are two types of clearing under the Electronic Clearing System.

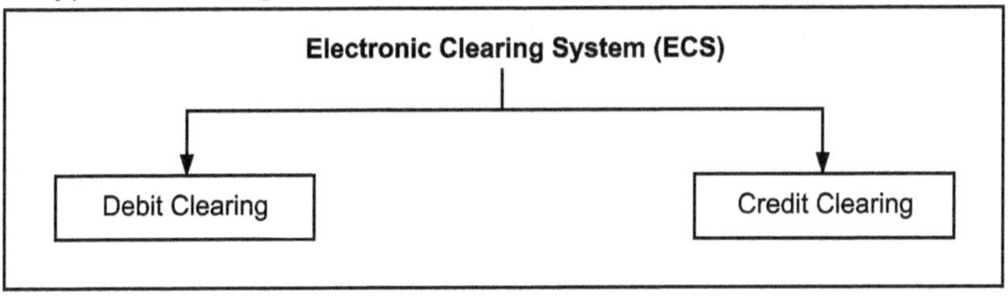

Fig. 3.6: Types of ECS

(i) Electronic Clearing System (Credit clearing):

- ECS credit clearing would have a single user who would wish to transfer money to multiple accounts. For example, an employer institution may want to credit salaries of its large number of employees. So this process involves multiple credits and a single debit.
- In this case, the user of the facility would very carefully prepare data about payment. This would be prepared using computer and later copied on the CD/floppy or any other removable electronic disk to hand over to his bank. i.e. the sponsor bank.
- This information given by the user would be accompanied with a mandate given to the clearing house to debit his account which he holds with the sponsor bank and credit the multiple accounts specified by him.
- The sponsor bank would hand over this data to that clearing house where the beneficiaries' bank is located.
- The clearing house would be authorised to debit the sponsor bank's accounts and credit the bank accounts of the beneficiaries.

(ii) Electronic Clearing System (Debit clearing):

- It is exactly opposite to credit clearing arrangement.
- Under the Electronic debit Clearing System there involves a single credit and multiple debits.
- This is useful from the viewpoint of the customers as large number of payments are collected through this system. For example, Telephone bills, electricity bills, payment of LIC premia etc.
- In this case, the user of the service is the institution/organisation that collects the payments, while the customer whose bills are being paid is the beneficiary.

- The clearing house, beneficiary's bank and the user's bank are the intermediaries. Before subscribing to this service the beneficiary is required to apply for this service by filling in a prescribed form.
- This form contains the information about the beneficiary's bank accounts. This form is infact a mandate given by a customer in favour of the collecting banker (i.e. the user's bank) to collect money from the beneficiary's bank.
- This mandate is an instruction given by the beneficiary to his bank to make payments whenever claims (for which the mandate has been given) on his account.
- So the preceding discussion makes it very clear that making payments of bills is facilitated through Electronic Clearing System.
- The user institution for example telephone exchange, gives the details of beneficiary's (customer's) account and amount to be debited.
- Compiling this data on a computer does this and copying the same on either a floppy or a CD, this is accompanied by a mandate given by the beneficiary.
- The clearing institution on the basis of the information available, debits the bank accounts of the beneficiaries and credits the account of the sponsor bank who in turn credits the account of its customer i.e. the user.

Advantages of Electronic Clearing System:

1. It saves time, money and energy involved in printing paper instruments.
2. The risk associated with loss of instruments in transit is done away with. The other formalities to be completed post loss of such instruments are also done away with.
3. Provided timely service to its clients.
4. The customers do not have to go to their branches to deposit these paper instruments.
5. In case of electronic debit clearing, customers do not have to wait in long queues. They infact are not required to go to the bill payment centres at all.
6. In case of electronic debit clearing system, the data about the amount of debit is known and accordingly cash arrangement can be made.

2. Real Time Gross Settlement (RTGS):

- RTGS stands for Real Time Gross Settlement.
- The RTGS system was introduced in India on March 26, 2004.
- It is a comprehensive and secured on line payment and settlement solution.
- It is set up, operated and managed by the Reserve Bank of India.
- Prior to the introduction of the RTGS we had what was known as the Net Settlement System, wherein the settlement of transactions was netted usually at the end of the day.
- But under the RTGS system the inter bank payment instructions are processed throughout the day.
- These instructions are settled on individual basis, transaction by transaction, throughout the day.
- Since, the settlement is continuous it is called real time and since the same is not at the end of the day, (where debits and credits are netted and the balance if any settled) but on individual basis, it is also termed as gross. This is how we derive the RTGS system.
- To be a part of the RTGS system banks need to maintain the RTGS settlement account with the RBI. This account is linked to the current account of the bank with the RBI.
- The current account of the bank would cross fund the RTGS settlement account of that bank. This funding would be for a day.
- The balances in the RTGS settlement account would be transferred back to the bank's current account that very day. This makes the transaction an intra day transaction and the RTGS settlement account an intra day account.
- Hence, it is expected of banks to maintain reasonable balances in the RTGS settlement account that they hold with the RBI.
- There are two types of funds transfer under the RTGS. They are:

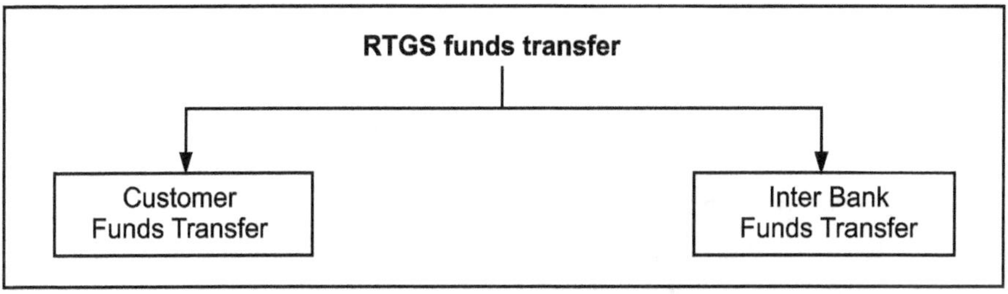

Fig. 3.7: RTGS Funds Transfer types

(A) Customer Funds transfer:

- Under the customer fund transfer facility an individual can use this facility to transfer money from his account to the account of the beneficiary.
- The customer funds transfer takes two forms viz. Outgoing, and Incoming.

(i) Outgoing Funds Transfer:

- For seeking the outgoing facility, a customer of a bank would have to submit an application form duly filled.
- He/She needs to fill in an application form which is meant for RTGS. Usually banks provide a common application form for various remittances such as DD/MT/TT and now RTGS.
- In case of an RTGS system the parties involved are:
  1. The originating bank, from where RTGS is sought.
  2. The customer, who wishes to send money through RTGS.
  3. The beneficiary, to whom the money is sent.
  4. The clearing institution, the RBI.
  5. The Receiving bank, who receives money on behalf of the beneficiary or where beneficiary holds an account. It is also known as the destination branch.
- The customer would fill in an application form and submit it to the originating bank.
- The application would mention the account number and name of the person along with the name and place of the bank where money is to be remitted.
- The customer (remitter) has to ensure that the bank on which he is drawing the RTGS should be an RTGS enabled bank.
- Unless banks get linked under the RTGS system, they can not access this facility. So the customer and the originating bank should confirm that the destination bank (branch) is a member of the RTGS.
- The originating branch would receive the payment from the customer in cash or debit his account as the case may be and then inform the destination branch online.

(ii) Incoming Funds Transfer:

- The destination branch would receive a message pertaining to credit the account of the beneficiary.

- On receipt of such a message, the authenticity of the same would be assessed and funds would be credited to the account of the beneficiary.
- The name and account number would be confirmed and the funds would be credited.

(B) Inter bank funds transfer:

- The inter bank funds transfer would also work the same way except for the fact that in place of an individual customer, there would be a bank.
- It is a bank to bank funds transfer.
- The system confers upon both its user and provider a number of benefits. Some of these benefits are as follows:
  (i) It minimises cost involved in transfer of funds.
  (ii) It maximises benefits by transferring funds quickly.
  (iii) Increases the velocity of circulation of money by transferring money in no time.
  (iv) Reduces risks associated with other paper based modes of transfer.
  (v) Provides liquidity, (cash) to the beneficiary on the date of transaction itself.

(iii) National Electronics Fund Transfer (NEFT)

- The National Electronic Funds Transfer is a nation-wide money transfer system which allows customers with the facility to electronically transfer funds from their respective bank accounts to any other account of the same bank or of any other bank network. Not just individuals but also firms and corporate organizations may use the NEFT system to transfer funds to and from. It was launched in the Year 2005.
- Funds transfer through NEFT requires a transferring bank and a destination bank. With the RBI organizing the records of all the bank branches at a centralized database, almost all the banks are enabled to carry out an NEFT transaction.
- Before transferring funds via NEFT you register the beneficiary, receiving funds. For this you must possess information such as name of the recipient, recipient's bank name, a valid account number belonging to the recipient and his respective bank's IFSC code. These

fields are mandatory for a funds transfer to be authorized and processed.

- NEFT transactions can be ordered anytime you want, even on holidays except for Sundays which are designated bank holidays. However, the transactions are settled in batches defined by the Reserve Bank of India depending upon specific time slots.

3.5.4.4 Advantages of EFT

- There are many advantages of using EFT through ecommerce website for financial transactions; some of them are as follows:
  1. Payments through EFT are much safer as compared to that of the cheques. There are no issues like lost or stolen cheques.
  2. Payments through EFT are quicker as compared to that of the cheques.
  3. Payments through EFT are quite convenient and easy.
  4. This is capable of eliminating the need to deposit and obtain the pay cheque or cash your pay cheque.
  5. Payments of EFT facilitate online baking though ecommerce website.
- Other benefits include lessen down of administration cost, greater security and increased efficiency

3.5.5 E-Payment systems

- There are several ways of transferring money from a bank or credit account to another user.
- Listed below are some of the modes of e-payments - Digital cash, Credit card, Debit card, e-cheque, smart card.

3.5.5.1 Digital Cash

- Digital cash (e-cash) or electronic money is a new concept in online payment system because it combines computerized convenience with security and privacy that improve on paper cash. Its versatility opens up a host of new markets and applications.
- E-cash presents some characteristics like monetary value, storability and irretrievability, interoperability and security. All these characteristics make it more attractive payment system over the internet.

- The predominance of cash indicates an opportunity for innovative business practice that revamps the purchasing process where consumers are heavy users as cash.
- E-cash is based on cryptographic systems called digital signatures. A pair of numeric keys work in tandem, one for locking (encoding) and other for unlocking (decoding).
- Messages encoded with one numeric key can only be decoded with the other numeric key, not otherwise, the encoding key is kept private and the decoding key is made public.
- E-cash is an electronic or digital form of value storage and value exchange that have limited convertibility into other forms of value and require intermediaries to convert.
- This payment system offers numerous advantages like authority, privacy, good acceptability, low transactions cost, convenience and good anonymity.
- But, this system of payment also has many limitations like poor mobility, poor transaction efficiency and high financial risk, as people are solely responsible for the lost or stolen.
- Electronic cash is susceptible to forgery. It is possible to create and spend forged e-cash.

E-cash Structure:

- E-cash structure could be identified as a string of bits that represents certain values such as reference number and digital signature. These could be used for the security purpose to prevent forgery and criminal use.
- But, the structure proposed by Wright needs some extension to make e-cash more secure.
- Therefore, the present model adds a digital watermark to e-cash structure to protect it from the illegal copy and forgery activities further, the model modified the structure of the reference number to support tractability as shown in the Fig. 3.8.

Currency	Value	Reference	Digital Signature	Digital Watermark

Fig. 3.8: E-cash structure

- The proposed e-cash structure is comparatively better than suggested by Wright, because security issue is given importance of top most priority in the present model.
- But, still there are certain concerns to be addressed for an electronic cash system. For example, who has the right to issue electronic cash? Can every bank issue its own money? If so how do you prevent fraud? And who will monitor the banking operations to protect consumers?
- Many of these concepts relate to the legal and banking regulatory aspects. However all these issues are beyond the scope of the study and therefore, cannot be included here. But, these issues must be addressed before establishing a complete e-cash based payment system.

E-Cash Processing:

1. Consumer buys e-cash from Bank.
2. Bank sends e-cash bits to consumer (after charging that amount plus fee).
3. Consumer sends e-cash to merchant.
4. Merchant checks with Bank that e-cash is valid (check for forgery or fraud).
5. Bank verifies that e-cash is valid.
6. Parties complete transaction.

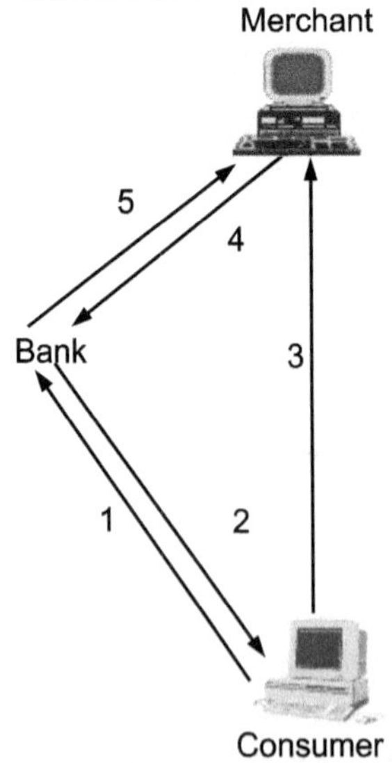

Fig. 3.9: E-cash processing

Advantages:

1. E-cash can be carried around.
2. E-cash is guaranteed by the government and does not normally lose its value in the short range.
3. E-cash is anonymous. Traders cannot normally say who gave a particular currency note.
4. E-cash is universally recognized as having value and accepted as legal tender.
5. Any person having cash can exchange it for goods or services without the help of a third party such as a bank.
6. Privacy of transactions is ensured because of anonymity.

Disadvantages:

1. E-cash is bulky.
2. E-cash is not safe. If you loses your purse you will be lucky to get your cash back.

3.5.5.2 Electronic Cheque

- Electronic cheques also known as Internet cheques or i-cheques.
- They are used to make electronic payments between two parties through an intermediary and not very much different from the current cheque processing system.
- Electronic cheques address the electronic needs of millions of businesses, which today exchange traditional paper cheques with the other vendors, consumers and government.
- The e-cheque method was deliberately created to work in much the same way as conventional paper cheque.
- An account holder will issue an electronic document that contains: the name of the financial institution, the payer's account number, the name of payee and amount of cheque.
- Most of the information is in uncoded form. Like a paper cheques e-cheques also bear the digital equivalent of signature: a computed number that authenticates the cheque from the owner of the account.
- Digital chequing payment system seeks to extend the functionality of existing chequing accounts for use as online shopping payment tools.

- Electronic cheque system has many advantages:
  1. They do not require consumers to reveal account information to other individuals when setting an auction.
  2. They do not require consumers to continually send sensitive financial information over the web.
  3. They are less expensive than credit cards.
  4. They are much faster than paper based traditional cheque.
- But, this system of payment also has several disadvantages. The disadvantage of electronic cheque system includes their relatively high fixed costs, their limited use only in virtual world and the fact that they can protect the users anonymity. Therefore, it is not very suitable for the retail transactions by consumers, although useful for the government and B2B operations because the latter transactions do not require anonymity, and the amount of transactions is generally large enough to cover fixed processing cost. The process of electronic chequing system can be described using (Fig. 3.10) and follow the following steps:

  Step 1 : A purchaser fills a purchase order form, attaches a payment advice (electronic cheque), signs it with his private key, (using his signature hardware), attaches his public key certificate, encrypts it using his private key and sends it to the vendor.

  Step 2 : The vendor decrypts the information using his private key, checks the purchaser's certificates, signature and cheque, attaches his deposit slip, and endorses the deposit attaching his public key certificates. This is encrypted and sent to his bank.

  Step 3 : The vendor's bank checks the signatures and certificates and sends the cheque for clearance. The banks and clearing houses normally have a private secure data network.

  Step 4 : When the cheque is cleared, the amount is credited to the vendor's account and a credit advice is sent to him.

  Step 5 : The purchaser gets a consolidated debit advice periodically.

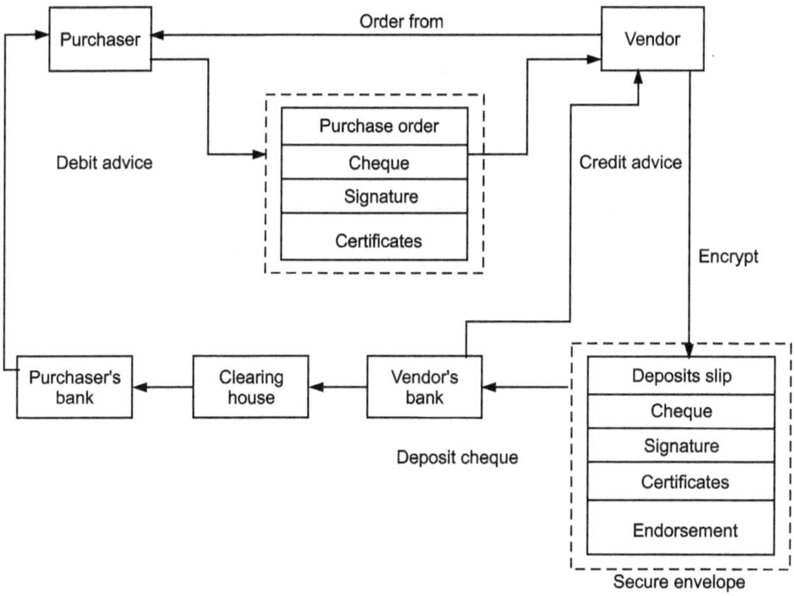

Fig. 3.10: Clearing Cheque payment electronically

- E-cheque provide a security rich internet payment option for businesses and offer an easy entry into electronic commerce without a significant investment in new technologies or legal systems.

3.5.5.3 Smart Cards

- A smart card, unlike a credit and debit card, is a card that is embedded with either a microprocessor with a memory chip or only a memory chip with non-programmable logic.
- While the microprocessor can add, delete and otherwise manipulate information on the card, a memory-chip card can undertake only predefined operations.
- Smart card contains some kind of encrypted key that is compared to a secret key contained on the user's processor.
- A smart card is any pocket-sized card with embedded integrated circuits which can process data. This implies that it can receive input which is processed and delivered as an output.
- Some smart cards have provision to allow users to enter a Personal Identification Number (PIN) code and these are being relatively common with billions of cards expected to use worldwide.
- These smart cards will emerge as the ultimate interface device for the mobile digital economy.

- These smart cards will hold your cash, ID information, house and office keys, subway tokens, all types of preference files and other information.
- Smart cards are receiving renewed attention as a mode of online payment. They are essentially credit card sized plastic cards with the memory chips and in some cases, with microprocessors embedded in them so as to serve as storage devices for much greater information than credit cards with inbuilt transaction processing capability.

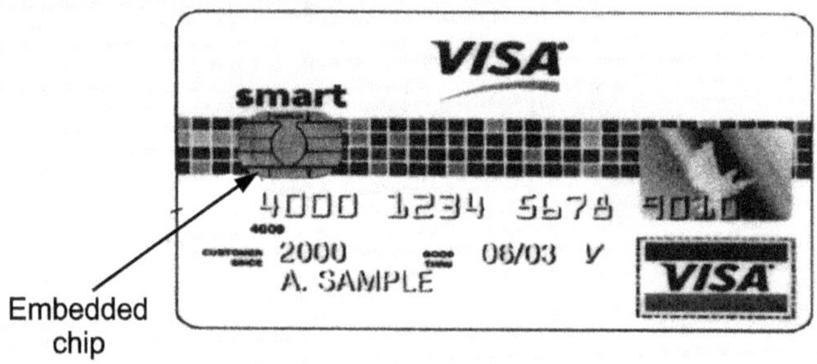

Fig. 3.11: A Smart Card

- Smart cards have been in use for well over the two decades now and have been widespread mostly in Europe and Asian Countries.
- Owing to their considerable flexibility, they have been used for a wide range of functions like highway toll payment, as prepaid telephone cards and as stored value debit cards.
- However, with the recent emergence of e-commerce, these devices are increasingly being viewed as a particularly appropriate method to execute online payment system with considerably greater level of security than credit cards.
- Compared with traditional electronic cash system, smart cards based electronic payment systems do not need to maintain a large real time database.
- They also have advantages, such as anonymity, transfer payment between individual parties, and low transactional handling cost of files.
- Smart cards are also better protected from misuse than, say conventional credit cards, because the smart card information is encrypted.
- Currently, the two smart cards based electronic payment system Mondex and Visa Cash are incompatible in the smart cards and card reader specification.

- Not knowing which smart card system will become market leader; banks around the world are unwilling to adopt either system, let alone other smart card system.
- Therefore, establishing a standard smart card system, or making different system interoperable with one another is critical success factors for smart card based payment system.
- The origin of smart cards can be traced to a frenchman named Ronald Moreno, way back in 1970.

Smart Card Standards		
• Open card Frame work	• Supported by Sun Microsystems, IBM, Oracle and Netscape	• It is a standard for NCs, emphasizes portability and personalization and adopts Java.
• Personal Computer Smart Card (PCSC)	• Proposed by Micro-soft and supported by Schlumberger Electronic Technologies	–
• Sun's Java Card API	• Endorsed by Citibank, Visa, First Union National Bank, Verifone	–
• Motorola Smartcard Systems Business Unit	• Contactless cards using radio	–

- The smart card technology is widely used in countries such as France, Japan, Germany and Singapore to pay for public phone calls, transportation and shopper loyalty programs.
- The basic idea has taken more time to catch on in the US, since highly reliable and fairly inexpensive telecommunication system has favoured the use of credit and debit card.

Smart Card Processing:

- Fig. 3.12 shows smart card processing steps are listed below:
  1. User opens account and receives smart card.
  2. User downloads tokens onto card.
  3. User inserts card in reader.
  4. Tokens are transferred from user card to vendor.
  5. Goods delivered.
  6. Vendor redeems tokens.

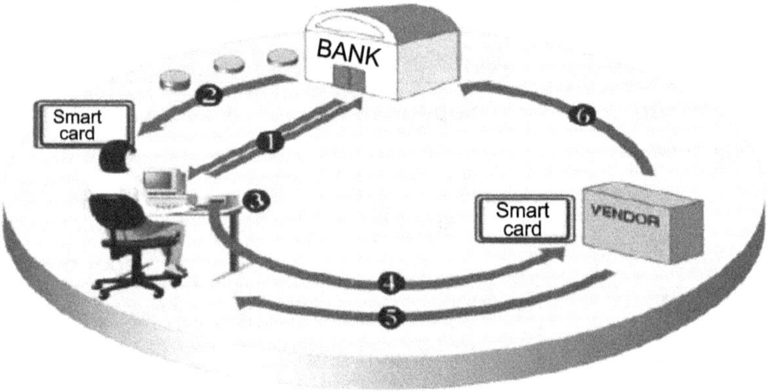

Fig. 3.12: Smart Card Processing

Types of Smart Cards:

- Smart cards are of two types i.e. Relationship based smart credit cards, and Electronic purses.
  1. **Relationship based smart card:** This card is an enhancement of existing card services and/or the addition of new services that a financial institution delivers to its customers via a chip-based card or other device.
  2. **Electronic purses:** These cards are wallet sized smart cards and embedded with programmable microchips that store sum of money for people to use method of cash for everything from buying food, photocopies etc.
- There are three categories of smart cards are:
  1. **An intelligent memory card:** It contains beside data, some built in logic, usually used to control access to the memory of the card. These cards have certain data processing capabilities.
  2. **A processor card:** It contains own microprocessor and an operating system. These cards can process and store data on their own.
  3. **A memory card:** It stores data. It will need an outside processor to access and work with this data.

- Two other types of cards are:
  1. **Contact-less cards:** They are passed near an antenna to connect via a radio signal. They have both a microchip and an antenna embedded. This allows the smart card to communicate without physical contact.
  2. **Contact smart cards:** They are inserted into a reader or validator for the data to be read. When the card is inserted into the reader, it transfers data to and from the chip via electrical connectors.

3.5.5.4 Credit Cards

- Credit cards is a plastic card having a magnetic number and code on it.
- It has some fixed amount to spend and customer has to repay the spend amount after sometime.
- History of credit cards starts in using credit cards in 1958-1960, when the Bank of America issued certain cards in California to select group of users to pay for products by participating merchants, without cash.
- The advantage of using credit cards is that users no longer have to carry cash to pay for a product.
- Earlier, a credit card was provided imprinting a number. This was sufficient and efficient to complete the transaction.
- Electronic processing was found necessary for online authorization and depositing functions.
- In the late 1990-1995, the internet provided an unlimited opportunity if businesses could get paid for products or services sold electronically.
- The credit card processing is simple and easy.
- After receiving from a customer details like his credit card number, name, expiration date, two more things should occur to complete the transaction.
  1. The electronic credit card information must be turned into an actual deposit at your financial institution.
  2. The credit card must be authenticated with the credit card firm or organisations so that you can receive an authorization number. This provides guarantee that the funds will be made available to you when you complete your deposits by ensuring the user of the card is not over his credit limited and that the card is not stolen.

Fig. 3.13: Master Card/Credit card

- Fig. 3.14 shows processing of credit cards payment.

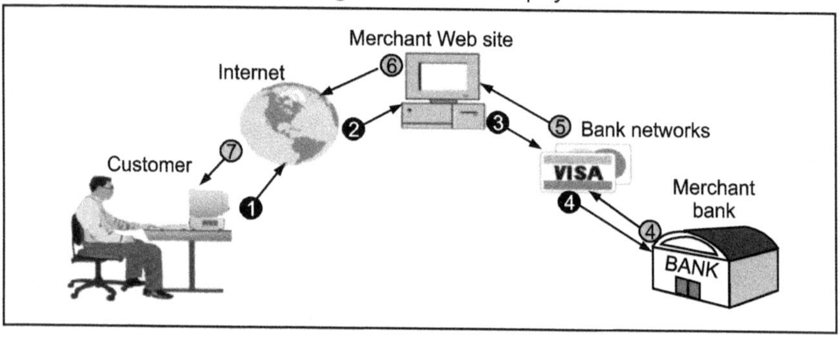

Fig. 3.14: Credit Card Payment Process

3.5.5.5 Debit Card

- This is one more form of Plastic Card.
- This is somewhat similar to that of a Credit Card. The only difference is that there is no credit facility available to the debit cardholder on his debit card.
- With the help of debit card the cardholder can withdraw and can pay for purchase of goods and services.
- On purchase of goods or services the cardholder's account is debited instantly.
- This card can be used only if credit balance exists in the account of the debit cardholder.
- This card is more suitable to those who wish to manage within their monthly income and who usually do not want to borrow.
- Hence, debit card is a card without any borrowing facility. Many banks issue ATM cum debit cards.

Advantages:

- Debit card facility carries the following advantages:
  1. Debit card gives twin benefits of cash withdrawal and cashless purchases.

2. The facility of cash withdrawal is available 24 hours a day and 365 days in a year through ATMs.
3. It offers its users the facility of convenient banking as withdrawals are possible from anywhere through the ATMs of the bank or any other bank.

Disadvantages:

- Debit card suffers from certain limitations. These are:
  1. Undisturbed power supply is needed for cash withdrawals through ATMs.
  2. Literacy in general and computer literacy in specific, among debit card users, is essential for general use of debit cards.
  3. Psychology of the people may limit working of debit cards. People on account of illiteracy may carry fear of using debit cards. This very fear about the ability to use the card, keeps many away from the use of debit cards.
  4. Debit cards do not have general acceptability. They are not widely accepted in all shops and hence cannot be taken as substitutes to money.
  5. Debit cardholders do not have any credit facility and are accepted only to the extent of balances in the account of the debit card holder.

Comparison of Electronic Payment Systems:

- Following table presents the comparison of various electronic payment systems.

Features	Online Credit Card Payment	Electronic Cash	Electronic Cheque	Smart Cards
Actual Payment Time	Paid later.	Prepaid.	Paid later.	Prepaid.
Transaction information transfer	The store and bank checks the status of the credit card.	Free transfer. No need to leave the name of parties involved.	Electronic cheques or payment indication must be endorsed.	The smart card of both parties make the transfer.
Online and offline transactions	Online transactions.	Online transactions.	Offline transfers are allowed.	Offline transfers are allowed.

contd. ...

Bank account involvement	Credit card account makes the payment.	No involvement.	The bank account makes the payment.	The smart card account makes the payment.
Users	Any legitimate credit card users.	Anyone.	Anyone with a bank account.	Anyone with a bank or credit card account.
Party to which payment is made out	Distributing Bank.	Store.	Store.	Store.
Consumer's transaction risk	Most of the risk is borne by the distributing bank, consumers only have to bear part of the risk.	Consumer is at risk of the electronic cash getting stolen, lost, or misused.	Consumer bears most of the risk, but the consumer can stop check payments at any time.	Consumer is at risk of the smart card getting stolen, lost or misused.
Current degree of popularity	Credit card organizations check for certification then total the purchases. Therefore, it can be used internationally, and is the most popular payment type.	Unable to meet financial internet standards in the areas of expansion potential and inter-nationalism.	Can not meet international standards, therefore its not very popular.	Credit card organizations check for certification then total the purchases. Therefore, it can be used internationally and is becoming more widely used.
Anonymity	Partially or entirely anonymous.	Entirely anonymous.	No anonymity.	Entirely anonymous, but if needed, the central processing agency can ask stores to provide information about a consumer.

contd. ...

Small payments	Transaction costs are high. Not suitable for small payments.	Transaction costs are low, suitable for small payments.	Allows stores to accumulate debts until it reaches a limit before paying for it. Suitable for small payments.	Transaction costs are low. Allows stores to accumulate debts until it reaches a limit before paying for it. Therefore, it is suitable for small payments.
Database safeguarding	Safeguards regular credit card account information.	Needs to safeguard a large database, and maintain records of the serial numbers of used electronic cash.	Safeguards regular account information.	Safeguards regular account information.
Transaction information face value	Can be signed and issued freely in compliance with the limit.	Face value is often set, and cannot be changed.	Can be signed and issued freely in compliance with the limit.	Can be deducted freely in compliance with the limit.
Real/Virtual world	Can be partially used in real world.	Can only be used in the virtual world.	Limited to virtual world, but can share a checking account in the real world.	Can be used in real or virtual worlds.
Limit on transfer	Depends on the limit of the credit card.	Depends on how much is prepaid.	No limit.	Depends on how much money is saved.
Mobility	Yes.	No.	No.	Yes.

3.5.5.6 Contactless Payment

- Contactless payment systems are credit cards and debit cards, key fobs, smart cards, or other devices, including smartphones and other mobile devices, that use radio-frequency identification (RFID) or Near Field Communication (NFC, e.g. Samsung Pay, Apple Pay, Google Pay, Fitbit Pay, or any bank mobile application that supports contactless) for making secure payments.
- The embedded integrated circuit chip and antenna enable consumers to wave their card, fob, or handheld device over a reader at the point of sale terminal.
- Contactless transactions can only be made when you are very close to a reader.
- Contactless technology is becoming more and more widespread, which means you're able to use it in a number of places. This includes various shops, restaurants, bars, cafes, and even automated services such as vending machines.

EMV Contactless Symbol on Payment Terminal

Contactless Card

Fig. 3.15

Advantages:

- Contactless payments are more secure than traditional magnetic stripe payments.
- Paying with a contactless payment card is faster than traditional payment methods.
- EMV chip card technology will likely make contactless payments more widespread.
- Contactless payment cards can be put in your mobile device with Near Field Communications (NFC).

Disadvantages:

- Few merchants use contactless payment systems. Not all customers are educated on how to use this technology. It can create confusion and frustration among users.
- Only customers who have e-payment apps on their mobile phone can use this technology. People can't leave home with their NFC-capable phone as they may need a magnetic stripe to make payment.
- If you lose your credit card, this can be a threat. The thief will not need to enter a PIN or sign a receipt to make purchases using your card until it is blocked. So, your account may be compromised.

3.5.6 Digital token based e-payment systems.

- The digital token based payment system is a new form of electronic payment system which is based on electronic tokens rather than e-cheque or e-cash. The electronic tokens are generated by the bank or some financial institutions. Hence we can say that the electronic tokens are equivalent to the cash which are to be made by the bank.

Categories of Electronic Tokens:

1. **Cash or Real Time:** In this mode of electronic tokens transactions takes place via the exchange of electronic currency (e-cash).
2. **Debit or Prepaid:** In this electronic payment system the prepaid facilities are provided. It means that for transactions of information user pay in advance. This technology are used in smart card, electronic purses etc.
3. **Credit or Postpaid:** These types of electronic token based on the identity of customers which issue a card, their authentication and verification by a third party. In this system the server authenticate the customers and then verify their identity through the bank. After all these processing the transaction take place. Example is E-Cheques.

3.5.7 Net Banking

- Net Banking, also known as online banking or Internet Banking, is an electronic payment system. It allows you to conduct many different types of transactions through the internet from the comfort of your home. Be it transferring funds to another bank account or checking the transaction statements, you can do them all and much more with the help of Internet Banking.

3.5.7.1 How to do Net Banking?

- To do financial transactions online, you need to log into your bank's website. You only need a personal computer, laptop, or even a mobile phone and an internet connection to log into your online banking account.
- Once you have logged in, you can easily use a host of financial services offered by your bank online without the need to personally visit the bank.

3.5.7.2 Features of Net Banking

- The customer using this facility can conduct transactional and non-transactional tasks including:
    - The customer can view account statements.
    - The customer can check the history of the transactions for a given period by the concerned bank.
    - Bank, statements, various types of forms, applications can be downloaded.
    - The customer can transfer funds, pay any kind of bill, recharge mobiles, DTH connections, etc.
    - The customer can buy and sell on e-commerce platforms.
    - The customer can invest and conduct trade.
    - The customer can book transport, travel packages, and medical packages.
    - The list of benefits a user can enjoy using internet banking is too lengthy, to sum up.

3.5.7.3 Advantages of Net Banking

1. The customers get permanent access to his/her bank anytime and anywhere.
2. Transactions are safe and highly secure.
3. Immediate funds transfer helps the user in time of urgent need.
4. It saves valuable time of the users.

3.5.7.4 Disadvantages of Net Banking

1. Need an account with an Internet Service Provider (ISP)
2. Security concerns, like "hackers" accessing your bank accounts
3. Original setup for bill paying time is time-consuming but will ultimately be a time-saver.

4. Switching banks can be more cumbersome online than in person
5. Must have basic computer skills and Internet knowledge
6. Must be comfortable using a computer.

3.5.8 Steps for Electronic Payment

- Online payment processing functions via a series of digital gateways. If a transaction meets the requirements of each individual gateway, it moves on to the next gateway. The last gateway is the merchant's bank, where the money is deposited.
- Steps of online payment processing:
  1. Customer makes purchase online
  2. Payment gateway encrypts transaction information
  3. Payment processor verifies transaction details
  4. Customer's credit card company approves or denies transaction
  5. Customer's bank authorizes approved funds
  6. Payment processor requests funds transfer to merchant account.
  7. Customer's bank transfers funds to merchant's bank.
  8. Merchant receives funds.

3.5.9 Payment Security

- Following are Security measures of online transactions:

1. **Ensure that your computer is defended against Internet threats:**
   - Help protect your online transactions by using firewall, antivirus, and antispyware software. Encrypt your wireless connection at home. Keep all software (including your web browser) current with automatic updates.
2. **Create strong passwords that are used effectively and changed regularly:**
   - Strong passwords are easy for you to remember but difficult for others to guess. They should be kept secret and should be changed regularly.
   - Use unique passwords for bank accounts and other important financial transactions. And avoid using the same password everywhere. If someone steals that password, all the information that the password protects is at risk.
3. **Look for signs that your information will be safe online:**
   - Before you enter sensitive data on a webpage, ensure that the site uses encryption – a security measure that helps protect your

data as it traverses the Internet. Signs of encryption include a web address with "https" (the "s" stands for "secure") and a closed padlock beside it (the lock might also be in the lower right corner of the window). And always double-check that you are at the correct website (for example, at your bank's site, not a fake one that has a similar URL).

4. Perform confidential transactions on a private and personal computer over a secure wireless network:

- Never perform any confidential transactions (especially any financial ones, such as paying bills, banking or shopping) on a public or shared computer, or on devices such as laptops or mobile phones that are on public wireless networks. The security is unreliable.

5. Find the web address yourself:

- Links in email messages, text messages, instant messages, and pop-up ads can take you to websites that look legitimate but are not. To visit websites, type the address yourself or use your own bookmark or favorite.

6. Use common sense:

- To help protect yourself against fraud, watch out for scams. For example, be wary of deals that sound too good to be true, alerts from your "bank" that your account will be closed unless you take some immediate action, notices that you have won a lottery, or a refusal to meet in person for a local transaction.
- Typically this kind of message, whether sent by computer or phone, is designed to entice you to visit a phony website where criminals collect your financial data. (If you doubt the message's authenticity, call the company.)
- Threats of payments system.

7. Security and the Basics of Encryption in E-Commerce:

- Security of systems resources generally follows a three-step process of Identification, **Authentication** and **Authorization**.
  - **(i) Identification:** It is a scheme established and maintained, whereby users are properly, consistently, effectively and efficiently identified before systems are accessed.
  - **(ii) Authentication:** Authentication is the digital process of verifying that people or entities are whom or what they claim

to be. The most common example of authentication is the use of a username and password to gain access to a system, network or web site. Authentication does not determine what tasks the individual can do or what files the individual can see. Authentication merely identifies and verifies who the person or system is.

Types of ecommerce authentication:

- **One-time password/Single sign on:** It is process where a user's password and information is used for logon and then, becomes invalid after a set time.
- **Two-factor authentication:** This requires two forms of authentication before access can be granted to a user.
- **Multi-factor authentication:** Multi-factor authentication requires that the user uses a user id, password combined with any other form of authentication method as smartcard or biometric. Security token - It is an authentication device that has been assigned to a specific user by an appropriate administrator". It uses what the user has such as, Passport, driver's license etc. to identify them. "Most security tokens also incorporate two-factor authentication methods to work effectively".
- **Keystroke dynamics:** It is an automated form of authentication based on something the user does. It authenticates the user based keyboard typing pattern.
- **Biometric:** Biometric based systems enable the automatic identification and/or authentication of individuals.

(iii) Authorization: Authorization is the process of giving someone permission to do or have something. In multi-user computer systems, a system administrator defines for the system which users are allowed access to the system and what privileges of use (such as access to which file directories, hours of access, amount of allocated storage space, and so forth). Assuming that someone has logged in to a computer operating system or application, the system or application may want to identify what resources the user can be given during this session.

- A secure computing environment would not be complete without consideration of encryption technology. The term encryption refers to the practice of obscuring the meaning of a piece of information by encoding it in such a way that it can only be decoded, read and understood by people for whom the information is intended. It is the process of encoding data to prevent unauthorized parties from viewing or modifying it.
- Encryption can be used to provide high levels of security to network communication, e-mail, files stored on hard drives or floppy disks, and other information that requires protection.

8. Encryption:

- **Encryption** is said to occur when data is passed through a series of mathematical operations that generate an alternate form of that data; the sequence of these operations is called an **algorithm**. To help distinguish between the two forms of data, the unencrypted data is referred to as the plaintext and the encrypted data as ciphertext. The security of encryption lies in the ability of an algorithm to generate ciphertext that is not easily reverted to the original plaintext.
- In a very simple example, encryption of the word "secret" could result in "terces." Reversing the order of the letters in the plaintext generates the ciphertext. This is a very simple encryption - it is quite easy for an attacker to retrieve the original data. A better method of encrypting this message might be to create an alternate alphabet by shifting each letter by some arbitrary number. This is known as a substitution cipher, a form of encryption that is still used in puzzle books today.

9. Keys:

- A key is a piece of information that allows only those that hold it to encode and decode a message. Keys come in many different forms such as passwords, numbers generated by an algorithm, digital fingerprints and even electronic devices that work like door keys. It is a series of numbers or symbols that are used to encode a message so that it can only be read by someone in possession of that key or a related key. A key allows both the sender and the recipient of the message to understand how the message has been encrypted and assures them that nobody else knows how it has been encrypted. It is the key that enables the recipient to properly decode the message.

- The individual who is sending the message communicates the key to the recipient of the message, allowing them to unlock it. One disadvantage of this system is that an attacker can decrypt the message if the key is intercepted. To protect the key, encryption can be used during communication or the key can be sent in a separate communication.

10. Decryption:

- Decryption is generally the reverse process of encryption. It is the process of decoding the data which has been encrypted into a secret format. An authorized user can only decrypt data because decryption requires a secret key or password. To make the data confidential, data (plain text) is encrypted using a particular algorithm and a secret key. After encryption process, plain text gets converted into cipher text. To decrypt the cipher text, similar algorithm is used and at the end the original data is obtained again.

11. RSA Algorithm:

- RSA is a cryptosystem for public-key encryption, and is widely used for securing sensitive data, particularly when being sent over an insecure network such as the Internet.
- RSA was first described in 1977 by Ron Rivest, Adi Shamir and Leonard Adleman of the Massachusetts Institute of Technology. Public-key cryptography, also known as asymmetric cryptography, uses two different but mathematically linked keys, one public and one private. The public key can be shared with everyone, whereas the private key must be kept secret. In RSA cryptography, both the public and the private keys can encrypt a message; the opposite key from the one used to encrypt a message is used to decrypt it. This attribute is one reason why RSA has become the most widely used asymmetric algorithm: It provides a method of assuring the confidentiality, integrity, authenticity and non-reputability of electronic communications and data storage.
- **Example:** Party A can send an encrypted message to party B without any prior exchange of secret keys. A just uses B's public key to encrypt the message and B decrypts it using the private key, which only he knows. RSA can also be used to sign a message, so A can sign a message using their private key and B can verify it using A's public key.

- **Cryptography:** It is the result of creation cryptographic methods, known as cryptosystems: There are two general categories for key-based encryption - symmetric and asymmetric.
    1. **Symmetric Cryptosystem:** Use the same key, or the secret key, to encrypt or scramble and decrypt or unscramble message.
    2. **Asymmetric Cryptosystem:** Use one key to encrypt a message and a different key to decrypt it. It is also called public key cryptosystems and rely on technology in which two keys, the public key and the private key are use to encrypt or decrypt data.
- Symmetric cryptosystem are the easier of the two implement, since one key required to encrypt and decrypt the message.

Common Uses of Encryption:

1. **Digital Certificate:**
    - Digital certificate are in effect virtual fingerprints, or retinal scans that authenticate the identity of a person in a concrete, verifiable way. A typical digital certificate is a data file or information, digitally signed and sealed by the encrypted using RSA encryption techniques, that can be verified by anyone and includes:
        - The name of holder and other identification information, such as e-mail address.
        - A public key, which can be used to verify the digital signature of a message sender previously signed with the unique private key.
        - The name of issuer, or Certificate Authority.
        - The certificate's validity period.
    - To create a digital certificate for an individual, the identity of the person, device, or entity that requested a certificate must be confirmed through combination of Personal Presence and Identification document. These certificates may be distributed online, which includes Certificate accompanying signature and Directory service. The decision to revoke a certificate is the responsibility of the issuing company.
2. **Secure Sockets Layer (SSL):**
    - It is introduced in 1995 by Netscape as a components of its popular Navigator browser and as a means of providing privacy with respect to information being transmitted between a user's

browser and the target server, typically that of a merchant. It is used by the most companies to provide security and privacy and establishes a secure session between a browser and a server.

- A channel is the two way-way communication stream established between the browser and the server, and the definition of a channel security indicates three basic requirements:
  - The channel is reliable.
  - The channel is private.
  - The channel is authenticated.
- This encryption is preceded by a 'data handshake' and has two major phases:
  - The first phase is used to establish private communication, and uses the key-agreement algorithm.
  - The second phase is used for client authentication.

Limits of SSL:

- While the possibility is very slight, successful cryptographic attacks made against these technologies can render SSL insecure.

3. **Secure Electronic Transaction (SET):**
   - It is more secure protocol. The difference between SET and widely used SSL is that SSL does not include customer certificate requiring special software called 'digital wallet' at the client site. (See will see more information in Section 3.5.10).
4. **Firewall:**
   - A firewall is a combination of hardware and software that sits between the internet and internal network of an organization to protect the network from outside attack. It can examine the data entering or leaving from the network and can filter the data according to certain rules, thus, protects the network from an attack. There are three main types of firewalls detailed as follows:

(a) Packet Filter Firewall:

- It uses a set of rules to determine whether outgoing or incoming data packets are allowed to pass through the firewall. For example, we can, as a rule, specify IP addresses of sending devices such that packets from these IP addresses are not allowed to enter the network. The Firewall would stop them from entering. A packet filter firewall is the simplest type of firewalls which operates at data link and network layers of the OSI model.

(b) Circuit Level Firewall:

- It is quite similar to the packet filter firewall. It also works on the basis of a set of rules for filtering packets but operates at the transport layer of the OSI Model so has greater functionality. As a rule, the higher the layer of OSI model where a firewall operates, the more sophisticated is the firewall. It can make packets sent from internal network to a destination outside the firewall appear as if they originated at the firewall. Thus information regarding hosts on the internal network remains secret. It can also determine whether TCP/IP connection between a host and a machine outside firewall has been properly established. Thus it can cut off any connection which has been hijacked by a hacker trying to pass through the firewall.

(c) Application Gateway Firewall:

- It operates at application layer of the OSI Model. It uses strong user authentication to verify identity of a host attempting to connect to the network using application layer protocols such us FTP. In contrast to packet filter firewall, it filters the requests rather than packets entering/leaving the network. It can block any outgoing HTTP or FTP requests. It can prevent employees of a company inside a firewall from downloading potentially dangerous programs from the outside.

3.5.10 Secure Electronic Transaction (SET)

- Secure Electronic Transaction (SET) was a communications protocol standard for securing credit card transactions over insecure networks, specifically, the internet.
- SET was not itself a payment system, but rather a set of security protocols and formats that enabled users to employ the existing credit card payment infrastructure on an open network in a secure fashion.
- SET is a system for ensuring the security of financial transactions on the internet.
- SET was supported initially by Mastercard, Visa, Microsoft, Netscape, and others. With SET, a user is given an electronic wallet (digital certificate) and a transaction is conducted and verified using a combination of digital certificates and digital signatures among the purchaser, a merchant, and the purchaser's bank in a way that ensures privacy and confidentiality.

- SET makes use of Netscape's Secure Sockets Layer (SSL), Microsoft's Secure Transaction Technology (STT), and Terisa System's Secure Hypertext Transfer Protocol (S-HTTP). SET uses some but not all aspects of a Public Key Infrastructure (PKI).

SET Protocol:

- SET is jointly designed by MasterCard and Visa with backing of Microsoft, Netscape, IBM, GET, SAIC and others.
- SET is designed to provide security for card payments as they travel on the internet.
- Participants in Set are cardholder (Customer), Issuer (Customer Financial Institution), Merchant, Acquirer (Merchant Financial), Certificate Authority.

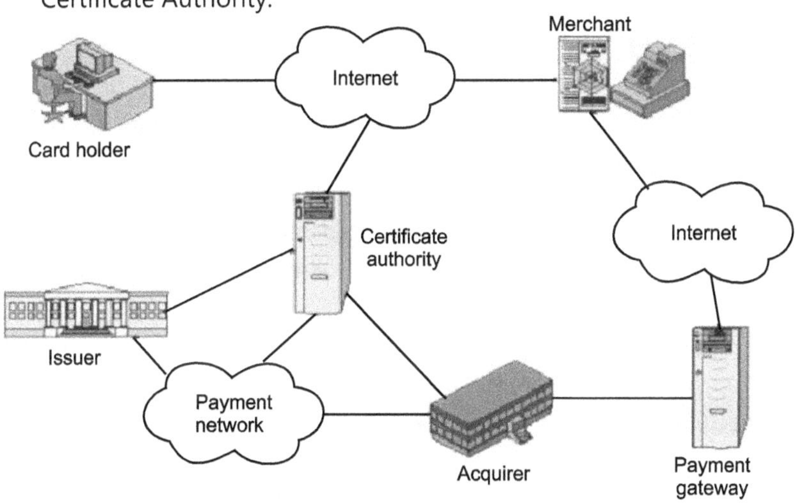

Fig. 3.16: SET protocol

- **SET specification:**
  - Uses public key cryptography and digital certificates for validating both consumers and merchants.
  - Provides privacy, data integrity, user and merchant authentication and consumer non-repudiation.

3.5.10.1 Definition

- Secure Electronic Transaction (SET), is a **standard** that will enable **secure** credit card transactions on the **internet**. SET has been endorsed by all the major players in the **electronic commerce** arena, including **Microsoft, Netscape**, Visa, and Mastercard virtually.

OR

- The secure electronic transaction (SET) protocol is used to facilitate the secure transmission of consumer credit card information via electronic avenues, such as the internet. SET blocks out the details of credit card information, thus preventing merchants, hackers and electronic thieves from accessing this information.

3.5.10.2 Advantages of SET

- It is an emerging technology has a definite security component that very clearly represents an advance in technology over SSL, and that any deficits that may be related to performance will quickly be rendered minor as hardware-based processing technology rapidly advance.
- SET is more secure protocol.

3.5.10.3 Business Requirement Addressed by SET

- SET addresses seven major business requirements:
    1. Provide confidentiality of payment information and enable confidentiality of order information that is transmitted along with the payment information.
    2. Ensure the integrity of all transmitted data.
    3. Provide authentication that a cardholder is a legitimate user of a branded payment card account.
    4. Provide authentication that a merchant can accept branded payment card transactions through its relationship with an acquiring financial institution.
    5. Ensure the use of the best security practices and system design techniques to protect all legitimate parties in an electronic commerce transaction.
    6. Create a protocol that neither depends on transport security mechanisms nor prevents their use.
    7. Facilitate and encourage interoperability among software and network providers.

3.5.10.4 How SET Works?

- Assume that a customer has a SET-enabled browser such as Netscape or Microsoft's Internet Explorer (IE) and that the transaction provider (bank, store, etc.) has a SET-enabled server.
    1. The customer opens a Mastercard or Visa bank account. Any issuer of a credit card is some kind of bank.

2. The customer receives a **digital certificate**. This electronic file functions as a credit card for online purchases or other transactions. It includes a **public key** with an expiration date. It has been through a **digital switch** to the bank to ensure its validity.
3. Third-party merchants also receive certificates from the bank. These certificates include the merchant's public key and the bank's public key.
4. The customer places an order over a web page, by phone, or some other means.
5. The customer's browser receives and confirms from the merchant's certificate that the merchant is valid.
6. The browser sends the order information. This message is encrypted with the merchant's public key, the payment information, which is encrypted with the bank's public key (which can't be read by the merchant), and information that ensures the payment can only be used with this particular order.
7. The merchant verifies the customer by checking the digital signature on the customer's certificate. This may be done by referring the certificate to the bank or to a third-party verifier.
8. The merchant sends the order message to the bank. This includes the bank's public key, the customer's payment information (which the merchant can't decode), and the merchant's certificate.
9. The bank verifies the merchant and the message. The bank uses the digital signature on the certificate with the message and verifies the payment part of the message.
10. The bank digitally signs and sends authorization to the merchant, who can then fill the order.

3.5.10.5 Steps (Stages) of SET Transaction

1. Card Holder connects to the ADFM website (www.adfm.org.my) via internet.
2. Card Holder clicks on 'Donation' button to donate. Enters Name as appeared on Credit Card, Billing Address and Amount to be donated.
3. Card Holder confirms the transaction and chooses to use SET. The Card Holder need to have a software called a SET e-wallet installed on his computer. The Card Holder will prompt download and install the software if it is not already present. The SET e-wallet will hold the Card Holder's Credit Card Details and is password protected. Upon Authorization by the Card Holder, the SET e-wallet will initiate a transfer of the Credit Card details encrypted in SET protocol to the Payment Server.

4. Payment server encrypts all info passed to it into SET and transmits the info to MEPS.
5. MEPS then passes the encrypted info to the Acquiring Bank (where ADFM has opened a Merchant Account)
6. Acquiring Bank will check with the card issuer for validation to prevent fraud.
7. Card issuer will inform acquiring bank of the authorisation status. Acquiring bank will pass the information to ADFM through the payment server via MEPS.
8. Upon Authorization received from Card Issuer, ADFM will be authorized to complete the transaction (carry out a capture). This will occur every 14 days to give the Acquiring Bank and Issuing Bank time to detect unreported fraud.
9. When ADFM captures the transaction, the card issuer will pay the amount into ADFM's merchant Account.
10. Card Holder is issued a monthly statement and pays for all transactions.

3.5.11 Introduction to Digital Signature and Digital Certificates

- Both Digital Certificate and Digital Signature are security measures and relies on digital cryptography.

3.5.11.1 Digital Signature

- A digital signature or digital signature scheme is a mathematical scheme for demonstrating the authenticity of a digital message or document.
- A valid digital signature gives a recipient reason to believe that the message was created by a known sender such that they cannot deny sending it (**authentication** and **non-repudiation**) and that the message was not altered in transit (**integrity**).
- Digital signatures are commonly used for software distribution, financial transactions, and in other cases where it is important to detect forgery or tampering.

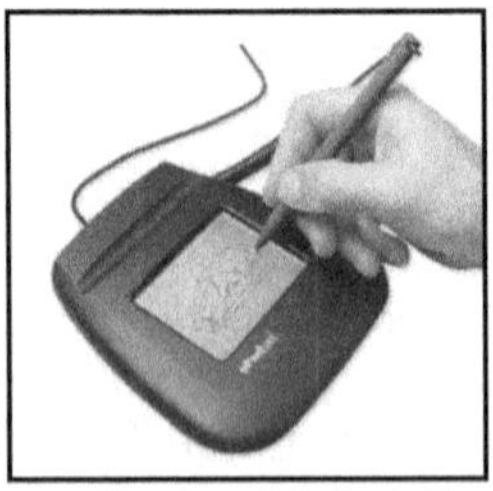

Fig. 3.17: Signing Digital Signature

Definition:

- A digital signature is an electronic signature that can be used to authenticate the identity of the sender of a message or the signer of a document, and possibly to ensure that the original content of the message or document that has been sent is unchanged.

OR

- Digital signature is a block of data that can be attached to documents like e-mail messages, word files etc.

OR

- Digital signature is a digital code that can be attached to an electronically transmitted messages that uniquely identifies the sender.

How Digital Signature Works?

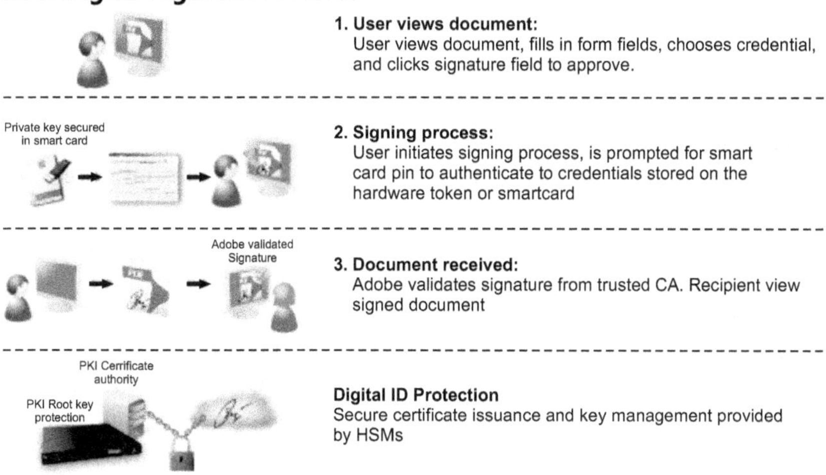

Fig. 3.18: Process of Digital Signature

Advantages and Disadvantages:

- The advantages of using digital signatures include:
  1. **Imposter prevention:** By using digital signatures you are actually eliminating the possibility of committing fraud by an imposter signing the document. Since the digital signature cannot be altered, this makes forging the signature impossible.
  2. **Message integrity:** By having a digital signature you are in fact showing and simply proving the document to be valid. You are assuring the recipient that the document is free from forgery or false information.
  3. **Legal requirements:** Using a digital signature satisfies some type of legal requirement for the document in question. A digital signature takes care of any formal legal aspect of executing the document.

- The disadvantages of using digital signatures involve the primary avenue for any business money. This is because the business may have to spend more money than usual to work with digital signatures including buying certificates from certification authorities and getting the verification software.

3.5.11.2 Digital Certificates

- A digital certificate establishes the credentials when doing business or other transactions on the Web.
- In simple words Digital Certificate is the attachment to an electronic message used for security purposes.

Definition:

- A digital certificate, also known as digital ID, is a computer-based file that verifies the credentials of individuals and institutions when accessing information and doing transactions online.

OR

- A digital certificate is an electronic credit card that establishes your credentials when doing business or other transactions on the web.
- The common use of a digital certificate is to verify that a user sending a message is who claims to be, and to provide the receiver with the means to encode a reply.
- Digital Certificate provides a means of proving your identity in electronic transactions; just like a driver's license or a passport does. You can present a Digital Certificate electronically to prove your identity or your right to access information or services online.
- A Digital Certificate is issued by a Certification Authority (CA) and signed with the CA's private key. It typically contains:
  - Owner's public key,
  - Owner's name,
  - Expiration date of the public key,
  - Name of the issuer (the CA that issued the Digital Certificate),
  - Serial number of the Digital Certificate, and
  - Digital signature of the issuer.

Components:

- The main contents of a digital certificate include the serial number of the certificate, version number of the certificate, signature algorithm identifier, issuer of digital certificate, public key information and validity period. These components are based on the standards established by the International Standards Organization (ISO) and adopted by the Internet Engineering Task Force (IETF) and the American National Standards Institute (ANSI).

Functions:

- The main function of a digital certificate is to ensure that a user sending a file or message is who claims to be. In addition, digital IDs provide a higher degree of security by encrypting messages so only the specified recipients can access the contents.

Applications:

- Digital certificates are part of the many security protocols implementted by software publishers, online businesses, e-libraries and virtually all computer-based applications that require authentication. For instance, most browsers store digital certificates of trusted authorities so that when you visit such websites, it verifies that you are visiting the right website and warns you when the certificate presented is invalid.
- Digital Certificates can be used for a variety of electronic transactions including e-mail, electronic commerce, groupware and electronic funds transfers.

Advantages and Disadvantages:

1. **Online Banking Advantages:** Many businesses rely on digital certificates for banking procedures. Online banking would not be possible without the use of digital certificates. According to Bank of America, transactions cannot take place until the digital certificate has been verified.
2. **Legal Advantages:** Digital certificates and signatures provide protection in legally binding situations. When sending email to a bank, for example, a digital signature will verify that the information came from you. When agreeing to legally binding requirements, digital certificates prevent you from becoming a victim of an impostor. In addition, digital certificates and signatures prevent the recipient from denying the receipt of information.
3. **Financial Disadvantages:** Businesses must purchase digital certificates from certification authorities. A certificate authority acts as a third-party issuer that ensures the acceptance of the certificate. Certification authorities typically require a subscription to their service, which requires monthly payments to continue the relationship. In addition, multiple certificates for different sites or purposes can become a costly endeavor.
4. **Technological Disadvantages:** When considering digital certificates, you need to factor in many areas of existing

technology. According to The Institute of Internal Auditors (IIA), "auditors should recommend that senior and IT managers consider the tool's ease of use, integration with the existing software platform, the company's product architecture, the security of the tool, vendor support, cost, and future flexibility before deciding which tool to implement." In addition, creating a platform that accepts all digital certificates is a difficult undertaking, and human carelessness may compromise the safety of login credentials.

SUMMARY

- Electronic data interchange is the concept of businesses electronically communicating information that was traditionally communicated on paper, such as purchase orders and invoices.
- Financial EDI is the electronic transfer of payments, payment-related information, or other financial documents in a standardized, machine-readable format.
- An e-payment system is a way of making transactions or paying for goods and services through an electronic medium, without the use of checks or cash. It's also called an electronic payment system or online payment system.
- An electronic funds transfer (EFT) is a transaction that takes place over a computerized network, either among accounts at the same bank or to different accounts at separate financial institutions.
- Types of EFT: NEFT, RTGS. NEFT (National Electronic Fund Transfer) The National Electronic Fund Transfer or NEFT is the simplest and most liked form of money transfer from one bank to bank. RTGS (Real Time Gross Settlement)
- The digital token based payment system is a new form of electronic payment system which is based on electronic tokens rather than e-cheque or e-cash. The electronic tokens are generated by the bank or some financial institutions.
- Digital Certificate is an electronic "password" that allows a person, organizaion to exchange data securely over the Internet using the public key infrastructure (PKI). Digital Certificate is also known as a public key certificate or identity certificate.
- Digital signature is a digital code (generated and authenticated by public key encryption) which is attached to an electronically transmitted document to verify its contents and the sender's identity.

- Credit Card The most popular form of payment for e-commerce transactions is through credit cards. Debit Card Debit cards are the second largest e-commerce payment medium in India.
- Secure electronic transaction (SET) was an early protocol for electronic credit card payments. SET was used to facilitate the secure transmission of consumer credit card information via electronic avenues, such as the Internet.

CHECK YOUR UNDERSTANDING

1. A ______ is an electronic file that uniquely identifies individuals and websites on the internet and enables secure confidential communications
   (a) Digital signature (b) Digital certificates
   (c) SSL (d) none of these
2. SET means ______ .
   (a) Standard Electronic Technology
   (b) Standard Electronic Transfer
   (c) Secure Electronic Transaction
   (d) None of these
3. EDI stands for ______ .
   (a) Electronic document interchange
   (b) Electronic data interchange
   (c) Express data interchange
   (d) Education data interchange
4. The principal electronic payment systems for ecommerce is ______ .
   (a) Credit card (b) Smart card
   (c) e-cheque (d) All of the above
5. Which of the following is a method of transferring money from one person's account to another?
   (a) credit card (b) electronic cheque
   (c) e-transfer (d) all of the above.

Answers

1. (b)	2. (c)	3. (b)	4. (d)	5. (b)

PRACTICE QUESTIONS

1. Answers the Following Question in brief:

1. What do you mean by electronic payment system?
2. What is an e-cheque?

3. Enlist various types of electronic payment system?
4. What is EFT?
5. Which are stages of SET?

2. Answer the Following Questions:

1. Write short note on financial EDI.
2. Which are technologies involved in EDI?
3. Explain any two types of EFT.
4. Write short note on Payment security.
5. What is net banking?
6. Explain in detail types of payment systems?

3. Write short note on:

Digital signature, Digital certificate, EFT, EDI, SET, Credit card, E-cheque, Digital cash, Smart card, e-Payment

4. Answer True or False:

1. EDI is a standard format for exchanging business data.
2. The EDI architecture divided into six layers.
3. MICR code line contains numbers.
4. RTGS is a type of EFT.
5. Smart card is type of e-payment system.

Answers

1. (T)	2. (F)	3. (F)	4. (T)	5. (T)

■■■

Unit **4**...

Introduction to M-Commerce

Objectives ...

- To understand the concept of M-commerce.
- To get information about advantages and disadvantages, applications of M-commerce.
- To know the difference between E-Commerce and M-commerce.

4.1 DEFINITION

- M-Commerce (mobile commerce) is the buying and selling of goods and services through wireless handheld devices such as smart phones and tablets. The term **Mobile Commerce** was originally coined in 1997 by Kevin Duffey at the launch of the Global Mobile Commerce Forum,
- It takes the help of the E-Commerce background and WAP technology. The use of wireless technology (WAP) to conduct sales of goods, provide services, make payments and other financial transactions, the exchange of information etc. is the basis of mobile commerce.

Various definitions of M-Commerce:

- M-commerce is the use of mobile devices to communicate, inform transact and entertain using text and data via a connection to public and private networks." ***- Lehman Brothers***
- "The core of mobile E-Commerce is the use of a terminal (telephone, PDA, PC device or custom terminal) and public mobile network (necessary but not sufficient) to access information and conduct transactions that result in the transfer of value in exchange for information, services or goods." ***- Ovum***
- "Business-to-consumer transactions conducted from a mobile device."(J.P. Morgan).
- "E-Commerce over mobile devices." ***- Robinson-Humphreys***
- "Mobile Commerce refers to any transaction with monetary value that is conducted via a mobile telecommunications network."

  - Durlacher

- "The use of mobile handheld devices to communicate, interact via an always-on high-speed connection to the Internet." ***- Forrester***
- "The use of wireless technologies to provide convenient personalized and location-based services to your customers, employees and partners." ***- Mobilocity***
- MobileInfo.com definition is closer to that of Ovum. It defines M-commerce as "Any electronic transaction or information interaction conducted using a mobile device and mobile networks (wireless or switched public network) that leads to transfer of real or perceived value in exchange for information, services or goods.

  - ***MobileInfo.com***

4.2 TYPES OF M-COMMERCE

- M-commerce can be categorized by function as mobile shopping, mobile banking or mobile payments.
  1. Mobile shopping allows for a customer to purchase a product from a mobile device, using an application such as Amazon, or over a web app.
  2. Mobile banking includes any handheld technology that enables customers to conduct dedicated transactions. This is typically done through a secure, dedicated app provided by the banking institution.
  3. Mobile payments enable users to buy products in-person using a mobile device. Digital wallets, such as Google Pay, allow a customer to buy a product without needing to swipe a card or pay with physical cash.

4.3 APPLICATIONS OF M-COMMERCE

- Other than the straightforward M-Commerce transactions of buying and selling of goods and services, they have so many applications. Let us take a look at a few examples,
  - **Mobile Banking:** Using a mobile website or application to perform all your banking functions. It is one step ahead of online banking and has become commonplace these days. It includes services like Mobile wallet, SMS based transactions, direct mobile billing, contact less NFC etc.
  - **Mobile Ticketing and Booking:** Making bookings and receiving your tickets on the mobile. The digital ticket or boarding pass is sent directly to your phone after you make the payment from it. Even in India now IRTC and other services provide m-ticketing services.

- **E-bills:** This includes mobile vouchers, mobile coupons to be redeemed and even loyalty points or cards system.
- **Auctions:** Online auctions having now been developed to be made available via mobile phones as well.
- **Stock Market:** Stock Market Reports and even stock market trading over mobile applications.
- **Entertainment and games:** Mobile terminal acts as a portable music player. Downloading ring tones has become successful M-Commerce application. Mobile phone manufacturers and wireless providers are making good money by selling different kinds of customized ring tones.
- Customers can play multi player games through mobiles. Mobile games are very popular with colorful displays and it generates good revenue.
- **Information:** Mobiles enable customers to get information like sport news or political news of their choice. For example, today through SMS, students are able to check their university results or public examination results.
- **Healthcare and medicine:** Wireless services are used in healthcare and medicine for billing, lab ordering, referrals, prescriptions and clinical decisions. For example, in United States, healthcare professionals are able to obtain patient information from any location by getting connected wirelessly to the hospital's information system. They are able to access the pharmaceutical information of patients and provide better patient care.

4.4 ADVANTAGES OF M-COMMERCE

- Mobile commerce offers a range of advantages to businesses both large and small. The number of people owning and regularly using mobile devices continues to grow, providing a large and growing – marketplace for a variety of goods and services.
- Following are advantages of M-Commerce:
  1. It provides a very convenient and easy to use the system to conduct business transactions.
  2. Mobile commerce has a very wide reach. A huge part of the world's population has a mobile phone. So the absolute size of the market is tremendous.

3. M-commerce also helps businesses target customers according to their location, service provider, the type of device they use and various other criteria. This can be a good marketing tool.
4. The costs of the company also reduced. This is due to the streamlined processes, now transaction cost, low carrying cost and low order processing cost as well.

4.5 DISADVANTAGES OF M-COMMERCE

- Following are disadvantages of M-commerce:
    1. The existing technology to set up an M-Commerce business is very expensive. It has great start-up costs and many complications arise.
    2. In developing countries, the networks and service providers are not reliable. It is not most suitable for data transfer.
    3. Then there is the issue of security. There are many concerns about the safety of the customer's private information. And the possibility of a data leak is very frightening.

4.6 SCOPE OF M-COMMERCE

- The **scope** of the Indian **mobile commerce** is expected to be having a progressive and aggressive growth in the future.
- Mobile commerce provides instant connectivity between mobile users irrespective of their geographical location and time of the day. With enormous growth of wireless and mobile technology and rapid penetration of mobile phones in developing countries worldwide, the scope of M-Commerce has increased manifold.
- The scope of mobile commerce is all pervasive and is gradually engulfing all aspects of lives of modern day citizens. Ranging from mobile banking, mobile browsing and mobile ticketing up to mobile marketing, mobile advertising and mobile computing.
- Mobile commerce is gradually becoming an integral part of both corporate world and common people. With the prices of mobile phone decreasing exponentially and the number of different mobile applications increasing enormously, more and more people will indulge in M-Commerce applications and soon it will become the preferred choice of the digital business world.

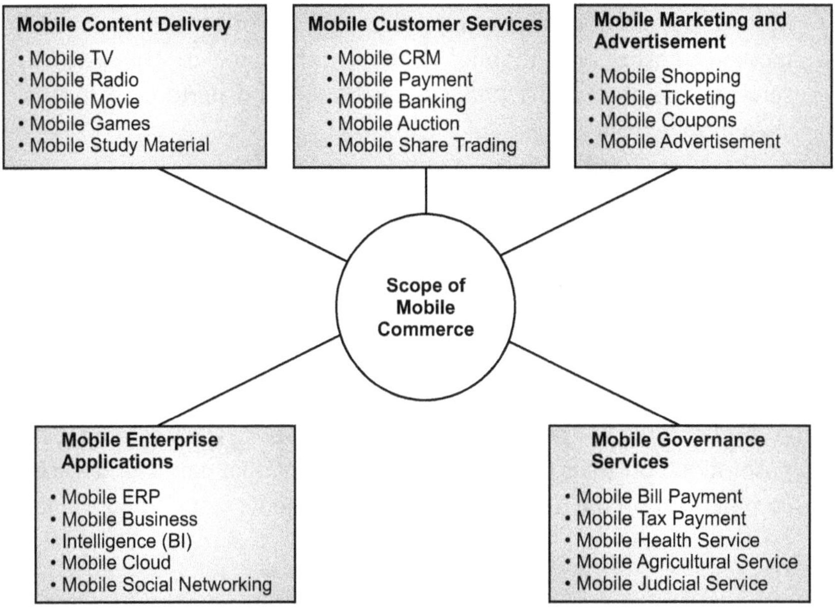

Fig. 4.1: Scope of M-commerce

4.7 PRODUCTS AND SERVICES OF M-COMMERCE

- The criteria for M-commerce services or products:
  - Limited but precise choice
  - Predictable availability
  - Does not require lengthy and in-depth decision making (appeal to impulsive buying behavior)
  - Convenience

Examples:

- The New York Times bestseller list meets all three criteria. It would be easy to purchase any of the listed books via a wireless device.
- Tickets to popular entertainment events, such as concerts, live theatre, movies, sports events, trade shows, public forums
- Micro-transactions: purchasing a fast food items, such as a soda pop from a vending machine;
- Payment of bills, banking, restaurant bill

Mobile Payment Applications:

- Mobile payment app is simply a mobile app acting as an alternative payment method where instead of paying with cash, check, or credit cards, a consumer can use a mobile app to make a payment.

- Mobile payment can also be referred as mobile money, mobile money transfer and mobile wallet, which cater to the payment services operated under financial regulation and performed from or via a mobile device.
- Credit card companies as well as IT companies such as Google, Apple and a number of mobile communication companies, have implemented mobile payment applications.
- Let's look at the most widely used Mobile Phone Payment Apps:

1. Google Wallet:

- Google Wallet is a mobile payment application developed by Google that allows its users to store debit cards, credit cards, loyalty cards, and gift cards among other things, as well as redeeming sales promotions on their mobile phone. Google Wallet can use near field communication (NFC) to "make secure payments fast and convenient by simply tapping the phone on any PayPass-enabled terminal at checkout."
- Instead of tapping your credit card on the NFC machine at the checkout counter, all you have to do is wave your smartphone or tap it on the machine to make your payments. It'll also be able to identify the credit card information linked on your Google account.

2. PayPal:

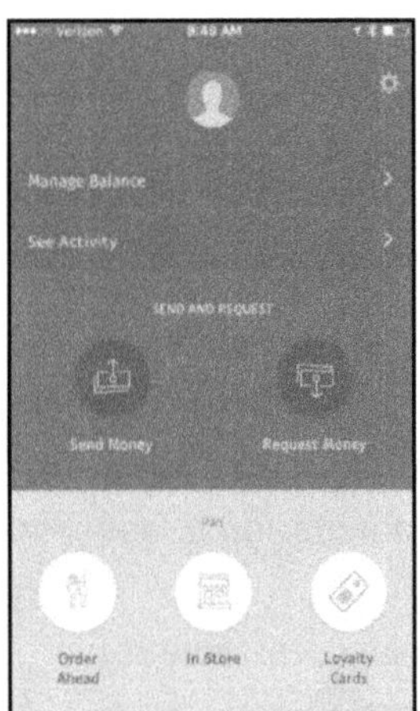

Fig. 4.2: PayPal App

- PayPal is one of the most accepted payment services on the planet. Lots of physical merchants and vendors are accepting payments through PayPal, no actual credit card needed. The PayPal app can use your location to determine what merchants and vendors around you let you pay with PayPal. Once you're at the checkout, just tell them you're paying with PayPal instead of cash or a card. You'll just have to enter your mobile number and PIN and you're good to go. PayPal just deducts the funds from whatever bank account or credit card you have linked.

3. **Google Pay:**

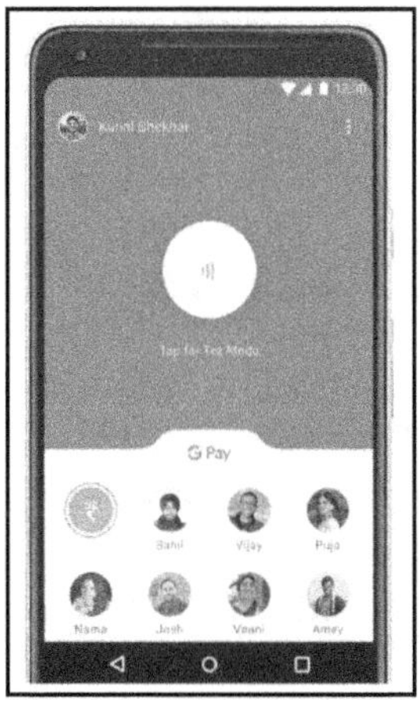

Fig. 4.3: Google Pay App

- Google Pay is a fast and simple way to pay online and in physical stores. With Google Pay, check out in hundreds of apps without having to enter your payment information. Google Pay Send, a peer-to-peer feature included inside Google Pay, has replaced the Google Wallet service. With Google Pay Send, pay anyone with an email addressor phone number. When you pay in stores, Google Pay shares an encrypted number (instead of your card details) with the merchant.

4. **PhonePe:**

- Today PhonePe is one of the leading payment apps. It uses the UPI Payment system for sending money and making payments for various services. It gives you the facility of the wallet as well. You can keep money in the PhonePe Wallet for faster transactions.
- The PhonePe is the subsidiary of Flipkart. That is why you can see this payment option in the Flipkart App. Now PhonePe and Flipkart Both are owned by Walmart.

Fig. 4.4: PhonePe App

- It has the following 3 outstanding features:
  - **(a) Quickest Fund Transfer:** The PhonePe has fewer steps for sending money. That is why money transfer through the PhonePe is fastest.
  - **(b) Easier Repeat Payments:** You can repeat a mobile recharge by going to the History page. You would also see the recent biller for the bill payment.
  - **(c) Effective Grievance Redressal:** It has incorporated the grievance along with the payments. You can very easily, raise a complaint or dispute. Often, you would find your answers immediately. The reversal of failed transactions is also very quick.

5. Paytm

- It is one of the most popular payment apps. In fact, Paytm has introduced the payment app to India.

Features:

- **(a) Widely Accepted For Payments:** You can see the Paytm QR code in most of the shops. All these merchants accept payment through the Paytm. As of now, Shopkeepers can get back money to their account without charges. This also helps in the acceptability.
- **(b) Various Services:** The Paytm has the most number of services. From school Fees to toll charges, You can pay for everything through the Paytm. It also gives facility of mutual fund and gold investment. You can also play games through the Paytm.

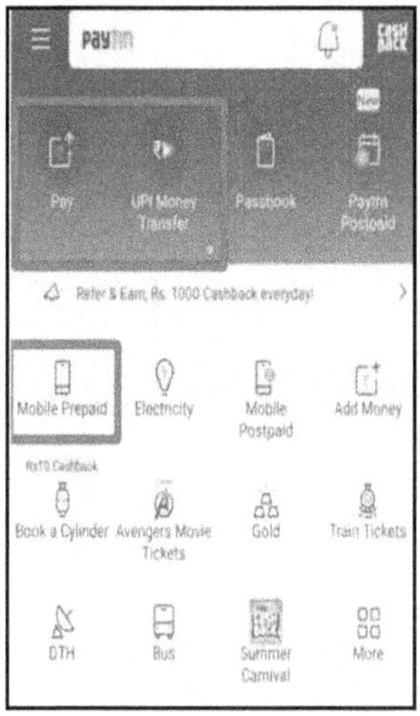

Fig. 4.5: Paytm App

(c) **Wallet and Payment Bank:** The Paytm has the seamless service of the mobile wallet and savings account. you can open a saving account in the Paytm Bank. Keeping money in this account would also give you interest.

You can use Paytm for small value transactions. The Paytm also gives you the feature of Paytm Postpaid which works like a credit card

4.8 DIFFERENCE BETWEEN E-COMMERCE AND M-COMMERCE

Sr. No.	Web World (E-Commerce)	Mobile World (M-Commerce)
1.	Access of internet is necessary for E-Commerce.	M-Commerce connectivity is launched as a wireless connectivity using mobile devices.
2.	Buying and selling products and services with the use of internet.	Buying and selling products and services with the use of mobile phones that have access to internet or cellular data.

contd. ...

3.	Requires devices such asccmputers, laptops, and so on.	Requires devices such as cell phone, iPads, tablets and so on.
4.	Platform used: Web Stores.	Platform used: Web stores (mobile version/web app) hybrid app, native app.
5.	Mobility is limited as you cannot carry computers everywhere. Even if you use laptops, you have to find the enough space to access it. Though it is portable, it is not a slight as mobile phones.	Since mobile devices are easy to carry it offers more mobility accessibility and convenience.
6.	Less costly as created on the web store platform and there is a usage of internet.	More costly as a mobile app is required and there is a usage of cellular data or internet.
7.	Since, it is applicable to the broader area, customization for each user is not possible.	Mobile devices are usually owned by individual so anyone can use the customized app to fulfill their business needs or personal.
8.	More complicated user interface and more functions available	Simple usage because all the functions are simplified.

SUMMARY

- M-commerce (mobile commerce) is the buying and selling of goods and services through wireless handheld devices such as smart phones and tablets.
- The major benefit of engaging in m-commerce is the sheer size of potential sales.
- M-commerce is recommended for every business irrespective of its type, scale, and size.

- Applications of M-Commerce are Mobile banking, Mobile Ticketing and Booking, E-Bills, Online auctions Stock Market Reports and stock market trading , healthcare and entertainment.
- The **scope** of the Indian **mobile commerce** is expected to be have a progressive and aggressive growth in the future
- Mobile payment app is simply a mobile app acting as an alternative payment method where instead of paying with cash, check, or credit cards, a consumer can use a mobile app to make a payment.
- E-Commerce is an umbrella term for selling and buying online, while mobile commerce, or M-Commerce, is a subcategory of ecommerce that focus on purchasing via mobile devices.
- Although the world of the web and the world of mobile devices are based on the same fundamental principles and aim to make people's lives easier, there are a few differences between ecommerce and m-commerce.

CHECK YOUR UNDERSTANDING

1. M-commerce stands for _____.
   (a) Mobile Commerce (b) Metropolitan Commerce
   (c) Modern Commerce (d) Mutual Commerce
2. Which is mobile commerce app.?
   (a) GooglePay (b) Paytm
   (c) Paypal (d) All of the above
3. Which is not application of M-commerce?
   (a) Mobile Banking (b) advertisement
   (c) e-bill (d) mobile ticketing
4. What year did m-commerce begin?
   (a) 1955 (b) 1977
   (c) 1989 (d) 1997
5. Disadvantage of m-commerce is that _____.
   (a) not most suitable for data transfer.
   (b) It is too expensive
   (c) possibility of a data leak
   (d) all of the above

Answers

1. (a)	2. (d)	3. (b)	4. (d)	5. (d)

PRACTICE QUESTIONS

1. **Answers the Following Question in brief:**
   1. Explain the concept of M-Commerce.
   2. Which are types of M-Commerce?
   3. What is meant by mobile payment application?
   4. Which are applications of M-Commerce.
   5. Write names of products and services offered by E-Commerce.
2. **Answer the Following Questions:**
   1. Explain the concept, benefits and application of M-Commerce.
   2. Write the advantages and disadvantages of M-Commerce.
   3. Write a short note: Scope of M-Commerce.
   4. Write features of Paytm App. in detail.
   5. Differentiate M-commerce with E-Commerce.
3. **Write short note on:**

   M-Commerce, E-Commerce, Mobile Payment App., Google Wallet, E-Bill, Mobile Ticketing, mobile banking. Google pay.
4. **Answer True or False:**
   1. Google Wallet is a mobile payment application.
   2. M-commerce is also known as M-business.
   3. Mobile banking is not application of M-commerce.
   4. E-commerce is a subcategory of M-commerce.
   5. Mobile commerce is E-commerce over mobile devices.

Answers

1. (T)	2. (T)	3. (F)	4. (F)	5. (T)

■■■

Model Question Paper

F.Y. B.Com. (Semester-II)

COMPUTER CONCEPTS AND APPLICATIONS – II

(2019 Pattern) (CBCS)

Time: 3 hours **Max Marks: 70**

Q.1 Solve the following:

(A) Select correct option for the following (any 5): **[5 × 1 = 5]**

(i) Which is not type of e-commerce?
   (a) B2B
   (b) B2C
   (c) C2C
   (d) all of the above

(ii) What does EPS stands for ______.
   (a) Electronic Payment System
   (b) E-mail Payment System
   (c) Electronic Payment Service
   (d) Ecommerce payment service

(iii) Which is not metrics of site usage?
   (a) Top entry pages
   (b) Top exist pages
   (c) Most visited pages
   (d) Testing web pages

(iv) M-commerce stands for ______.
   (a) Metropolitan Commerce
   (b) Mobile Commerce
   (c) Modern Commerce.
   (d) Mutual Commerce

(v) The principal electronic payment systems for ecommerce is ______.
   (a) Credit card
   (b) Smart card
   (c) Debit card
   (d) All of the above

(vi) Which is not Mobile Commerce App. for online payment?
   (a) Google Pay
   (b) Paytm
   (c) Paypal
   (d) Firefox

(B) Answer True or False of following (any 5): **[5 × 1 = 5]**

(i) Doing business online is known as E-commerce.
(ii) E-mail Marketing is a type of E-Marketing.
(iii) M-commerce is a subcategory of E-commerce.
(iv) Linux is a Mobile Payment application.
(v) NEFT is not a type of Electronic Fund Transfer.
(vi) M-commerce is also known as M-business.

Q.2 Attempt any four of the following: **[4 × 5 = 20]**

(i) Explain any two E-commerce types?
(ii) What is E-marketing?
(iii) Write applications of M-commerce.
(iv) Explain types of EFT?
(v) Write advantages of Debit card.

Q.3 Attempt any four of the following: **[4 × 5 = 20]**

(i) Write the difference between electronic cash and electronic cheque?
(ii) What is contactless card?
(iii) How to define financial EDI?
(iv) What is C2C e-commerce?
(v) Which are technologies used in E-commerce systems?

Q.4 Write short note on (any 5) **[5 × 4 = 20]**

(i) B2B E-commerce
(ii) Electronic Data Transfer
(iii) Electronic Payment system
(iv) CRM
(v) Mobile-commerce
(vi) PayTm

■■■

www.ingramcontent.com/pod-product-compliance
Lightning Source LLC
LaVergne TN
LVHW011812181026
850499LV00040BA/1360
9789389686555